The Last Violet: Mourning My Mother

Lois Tschetter Hjelmstad

Mulberry Hill Press
Englewood, Colorado

Mulberry Hill Press
2710 South Washington Street, Suite B
Englewood, Colorado 80110-1679

Editorial assistance:	Dianne Lorang, The Write Help, LLC
	Chris Roerden
Cover design:	Robert Howard
Page design:	Carol Magin Stearns

The following was originally published as indicated:
"My Voice Swept Away on the Wind" in *Fine Black Lines: Reflections on Facing Cancer, Fear and Loneliness*, page 6

Publisher's Cataloguing in Publication

Hjelmstad, Lois Tschetter
    The last violet: mourning my mother / Lois Tschetter Hjelmstad
    p.   cm.
    Includes index.
    Library of Congress Control Number: 2002100232
    ISBN 0-9637139-7-3
    1. Hjelmstad, Lois Tschetter. 2. Bereavement—Psychological aspects. 3. Parents—Death. 4. Grief. 5. Terminally ill—Family relationships. I. Title

155.9'37—dc21

Printed in the United States of America
First Printing 2002

To my mother—
I miss her more
than I could have imagined

To my sister, Jan, and brother, Nick,
who have lived this story with me

To my children
Karen, Robert, Keith, and Russell,
who will carry on her legacy—
and mine

My Voice Swept Away on the Wind

I had a collie
when I was three.

Mother let me wander freely
through the fields—

knowing Collie would protect me
and bring me safely back.

One day Collie went out alone
and didn't come home again.

I remember standing in the doorway
    calling, calling, calling
        my voice swept away
           on the wind. . .

A neighbor later told Dad
that he saw my dog stray near his sheep
and shot her.

Sometimes I think of Collie—
understanding clearly now
how things can be taken from you.

And still I hear myself
    calling, calling, calling
        my voice swept away
           on the wind. . .

Contents

*F*oreword

I will never forget the first time I met Lois Hjelmstad. She had given a talk about her cancer experience. Afterward, she was surrounded by a throng of women eager to shake her hand and sign their copies of her book, *Fine Black Lines: Reflections on Facing Cancer, Fear and Loneliness*.

This wonderful little book wasn't on anyone's bestseller list, yet for these women who had faced cancer, it was their scripture, and Lois, their inspiration. Here was a woman who struggled with cancer and spoke of it not with the coldness of a clinician or the somberness of a preacher, but, the heartfelt reality of someone who had been through it. She told of her experiences with wit, wisdom, and with remarkable insight.

She brings these amazing gifts to her new work, *The Last Violet: Mourning My Mother*. The next time I see Lois, I am sure she will again be surrounded by those who want to thank her for capturing yet another aspect of life in her wonderfully unique and moving way. Lois is a gifted storyteller and we all benefit by her loving words.

—Fred Silverman, New York producer of award-winning PBS documentaries such as: *Healthcare Crisis: Who's at Risk* and *Living with Cancer: A Message of Hope*

Acknowledgments

My heartfelt gratitude to Peggy Cole, Ph.D., Chair of the English Department at Arapahoe Community College, for helping me find the heart of this book and lending me the courage to write what was true. Her friendship gave me the strength to finish it when I wasn't sure I could.

My deep appreciation also to:

- my editors—Dianne Lorang of The Write Help for her support, suggestions, and faith, and Chris Roerden for her careful editing and constructive criticisms
- the persons who read the manuscript, offering encouragement and ideas—Alan Canner, Madelyn Case, Jeanne Currey, Joan Eichelberger, Walter and Carol Friesen, Joy De Groot, Caron B. Goode, Ralph and Mary Jo Hjelmstad, Thom Kelly, Judy Macomber, Martha Millsap, June Nelson, Pat Patterson, Marge Reed, Vern and Marilyn Rempel, Ann Showalter, Fred Silverman, and Carol Swartzendruber
- my physicians, Arthur Ziporin, M.D. and Martin Rubinowitz, M.D., who endeavored to keep me healthy enough to write
- my brother and sister for providing a sounding board, for helping me delve into our memories in a search for the truth of our lives together, and for joining me in mourning our mother
- my children and their mates, who talked with me, supported me, provided reassurance, and loved me through the process

And my undying devotion to my husband, Les, without whose care and confidence, I couldn't have written this or any book.

The Last Violet:
Mourning My Mother

The author's mother at age 21

The Sadness of Her Smile

A Daughter's Tale

*O*nce upon a time, there was a little girl who loved to play house. She hosted many tea parties, drinking the tea with her little finger lifted daintily into the air—just as her mother did. She cared for her dolls, diapering and feeding them—just as her mother cared for her little brother.

She had only two dolls—a bald baby doll and a new Christmas doll with beautiful blond hair—so the parties were quite intimate, unless Teddy Bear and Lambie joined them. She loved both the dolls, but when she paid attention to the new one, she always worried that the old one might feel displaced.

One afternoon, before it was time for the party, the little girl awoke from a nap. She called and called for her mother. She couldn't get out of her crib. The shades in her room were drawn, and she could barely see her dolls waiting at the small table in the scary dark.

> *Your mother is ill, they said.*
> *She has an ear infection, they said.*
> *Don't bother her, they said.*
> *She can't hear you, so be quiet, they said.*
> *You must be a big, brave girl, they said.*

The little girl was frightened that whole week—until her mother was well and the world felt safe again.

As the years went by, her mother taught her how to keep a perfect house, how to keep children well clothed and well fed, and eventually how to be a good grandmother. Her mother also tried to teach her how to raise African violets, but they always died, no matter how hard she tried.

Other things she had to learn on her own—how to juggle both a family and a career as a piano teacher; how to deal with aging parents; and how to cope with her own breast cancer, chronic fatigue syndrome (CFS), and osteoporosis.

But even though she had learned to be a woman, in some ways she remained her mother's little girl—trying to please, seeking her advice, considering even her most painful admonitions—until one day, her mother was diagnosed with cancer, just as she had been.

She didn't want to let her mother down and vowed to do whatever she had to do. She washed her mother and diapered her and stroked her forehead and tried to guess what she needed. She returned again and again, no matter how hard her mother tried to push her away—along with her dreadful knowledge of cancer.

And on that last day, the daughter held her mother's hand until she fell asleep. Tears tumbled down her cheeks as she combed her mother's silver hair and arranged the slender hands across the cold, dead heart.

At night, in the scary dark, she called and called for her mother. Sometimes she pretended to be a brave woman.

Sometimes she almost suffocated with grief. . .

Sunday Morning, Long Ago

The stained glass window
caught the rays of sun
flashing glints of red, yellow, blue

The form of Jesus
praying by a rock
dominated the picture

His face looked sad—
I nestled close to my mother,
sorrow played across her face, too

She looked neither left nor right
except to frown slightly
when I moved or made a rustle

I felt a chill and slid closer—
burrowing my face into her furry collar,
searching for warmth, safety, love

The gentle fragrance of her body
reached out to comfort me

The sadness of her smile
left me searching. . .

On My Childhood

I think about that Sunday morning so long ago. Why did her face look sad? What chilled my four-year-old heart? Why do my childhood recollections of my mother overwhelm me with a sense of sadness and disapproval, a feeling of my not quite measuring up to the standard she set for me, her firstborn?

Our relationship always hovered between connection and conflict.

For the first four years of my life, I was an only child and the only grandchild on either side, too. Undoubtedly, I was as adored and pampered as those times would allow, and I loved my mother dearly.

But when my brother, Nicky—"such a sweet baby," "a son, at last!"—entered our lives, I became a defiant four-year-old. When my "darling little sister," Jannie, was born, I was an awkward eight-year-old—expected to set a good example.

Like most firstborn children, I paved the way for my younger brother and sister. But I was also caught between the very different temperaments of my parents. With the soul of a scientist, my father continually quested after the truth and wanted to examine every side of an issue. Mother often said he just argued for argument's sake. She usually became silent and disapproving at the least hint of conflict. But she wasn't always able to contain the anger that she tried to repress.

I attempted to balance my increasingly inquisitive nature with my yearning for Mother's love and approval.

I still painfully recall that Good Friday when I felt I had lost not only her love and approval, but also God's.

As I walked up the center aisle of the church, my family following, I started to enter the pew that felt just right to me on that sacred day. When I resisted Mother's efforts directing me to another row, she withered me with one of her looks, and said, "Here we are in the Lord's House and you are arguing, just before we take communion." I felt the way Peter must have felt when he heard the cock crow the third time. I had confirmed what she had said just a few weeks before, "You'd even argue with me in church. You are just like your father."

For most of my life, when she was displeased with me, she said disparagingly, "You're just like your father."

Yet when my parents disagreed, I was the peacemaker. When they sniped at one another, which was much more common than open disagreement, I didn't know what to do, but still felt responsible. I always tried to smooth things over.

Although I have some very pleasant memories—picnics, trips to the library, birthday parties, and bedtime stories every night—I couldn't get past an overriding feeling that it was necessary for me to hold the two of them together, and the belief that I wasn't as good as I should be.

And I couldn't smooth over the summers. Since my dad was a schoolteacher whose meager pay could not carry us through the summer, our family spent every vacation on a farm with grandparents. Some summers we spent with Dad's parents in South Dakota; some, with Mother's parents in Colorado. And some we divided between them. My grandparents were good about taking us in and feeding us. Dad worked in the harvest fields to supplement our income.

We children thought the trips were lots of fun. I can still picture Dad driving along, and hear him singing in his beautiful tenor voice. I can still hear Mother's voice as she complained about having to move every spring and fall, having to pack all our belongings each time.

Both of my parents struggled to provide a comfortable life for us. Although Mother had taught school the winter before they were married, she would have considered it unseemly in the 1930s to continue after they were married. Dad worked hard teaching high school science during the school year. Mother kept all of us well fed and well clothed. She canned bushels of fruit when we returned to our rental house in the fall; she baked cinnamon rolls and bread every Saturday; she carefully took apart old garments given to her by friends and made me lovely coats and dresses; she scrubbed and cleaned the house until everything was spic-and-span.

She liked homemaking and kept striving to make her house and her children fit the model in *Ladies Home Journal*. On her sixtieth wedding anniversary, she told my daughter that all she had ever wanted was to be a flawless mother, raise well-behaved children, and keep a beautiful home.

Although everyone complimented Mother on her children, her home, her cooking, and the paintings she did, she was never satisfied with her efforts. It was hard for her to find or express happiness. She was always *waiting*: "Everything will be perfect as soon as. . . ."

I think she was more contented during the last decade of her life, but she never seemed truly happy, except the times when her only sister, fifteen years younger, visited from California. And she did seem to thoroughly enjoy the day when all the children and grandchildren came together to commemorate Mom and Dad's fiftieth wedding anniversary.

She never seemed to understand that people could love each other—and themselves—in spite of their flaws. Perhaps that's because she never felt truly loved herself.

My grandmother was not a happy person, either. A stoic German pioneer, she was very strict and unbending much of the time, convinced that the world was painted in black and white. Right was right; wrong was wrong. Neither my aunt nor I remember seeing any affection between Grandpa and Grandma.

Unhappiness was part of Mother's heritage, unhappy marriage a norm. Dad and Mother each entered their marriage at a disadvantage—she on the rebound, having been jilted, and he marrying her against his mother's wishes. I think they loved each other in their own way, but I'm not sure they really liked one another. Sometimes I'm not sure she liked me.

Do any of us ever really know why our mothers are the way they are? All I can know is how I feel about her and about my regrets concerning our relationship.

Fight to the Finish

It always seemed
like a battle, a contest of sorts,
trying to win her love

Surely Love was there

Why did it have
to be wrested
from its hiding place?

The Care and Feeding
of Violets

*A*long with her cooking and homemaking skills, my mother was an artist. In college, she had done charcoal drawing and watercolor. After her children were grown, she studied oil painting. She had a real eye for beauty in any form.

Mother loved flowers. Her favorites were African violets. After we children had left home, a friend gave Mother a violet and she fell in love with it. She discovered she had a knack for putting the little leaves in a soil medium and propagating the plants. Other friends brought additional varieties. Sometimes Dad would buy one. The garden on the windowsill grew. For the last thirty years of her life, she always had at least twenty violets on a special windowsill built specifically for that purpose in her dining room.

Mother tenderly watered and fed them. She carefully scraped scale from their stalks and cured their diseases, exactly according to the book.

Granted, their little faces were sweet and innocent, but I often wondered why she loved her violets as much as she did. When I asked my aunt if she had any idea, she said, "Maybe it was because she was in charge of their care and feeding. Your dad didn't leave a lot to her control. And I think it was also because they were something she could nurture. They were like little children to her. She liked to talk to them—and they never talked back."

There is no denying, the violets heard my mother's voice and responded—single flowers, double flowers, a riot of pink, purple, and white colors, profuse and beautiful.

Although I never asked for one, Mother occasionally sent a violet home with me. I guess I didn't have the time and patience to care for them properly. I was wrapped up in my family, my students—my own interests. When my violets died, in rather short order, Mother chided me, "Why do you always kill them? You have to *love* them. You have to *talk* to them."

She despaired at my dead violets.

Little in Common

My grandmother loved flowers, just as my mother did. Even on her austere homestead on the arid plains of eastern Colorado, red geraniums, moss roses, and morning glories flourished under her care. The love of flowers was one of the few things my mother and her mother seemed to have in common.

They had an unusually difficult time getting along—everyone noticed. Anything Grandma Kate said, Mother refuted. They couldn't agree on anything. Sometimes they wouldn't even make an effort to be civil to each other, even though, after we no longer stayed on the farm in the summer, they didn't see one another often.

My mother was very quick. Grandma was much slower, her movements more deliberate. Mother loved to cook and Grandma didn't cook at all if she could help it. Our main meal on the farm usually consisted of bread, butter, jelly, milk, and occasionally, a soft-boiled egg.

My mother hated any kind of a trip; Grandma would travel anywhere at the drop of a hat. Grandma tatted lace; Mother knitted and crocheted.

Grandma never grew African violets. Perhaps that's why violets were Mother's favorite flowers.

I loved both my grandmother and my mother. But once again, I was in the awkward position of trying to smooth things over between two people I loved.

The Care and Feeding
of Mother

*O*ne thing I remember clearly about my childhood is a pervading sense of shame—"Shame on you" for playing when I was supposed to be napping, for spilling my milk, for scuffing my black patent leather shoes, for hollering out the front door, asking an entire neighborhood what f—u—c—k meant. (I always have liked words.)

One day, when I was seven or eight, I was walking to school with my father, playing with words, making rhymes. For some reason, I was rhyming words that ended in "it"— "bit, fit, hit, kit, lit, pit, shit—." I stopped cold. Daddy said, with a small smile, "You didn't mean for that to slip out, did you?" Thank God for the small smile.

That slip would have horrified Mother, much as the inquiry regarding the letters "f—u—c—k" did. "Where did you learn such language? Surely you know better. Why are you yelling out the door, anyway?"

My brother, my sister, and I were taught early on how we were expected to behave, and we learned to dread the "shame on you" when we didn't remember. To this day, my cheeks burn with disgrace and humiliation when I forget an appointment or make a careless remark.

We also learned that we must be careful with Mother. She was easily upset. We found out that simple transgressions might send her to her knees to pray for us, that conflict often dissolved her into tears, that talking back risked a cold, sad look.

Often it seemed as if we were walking on eggshells.

Perhaps we found it difficult to talk with Mother about things that mattered, because she would somehow miss the cry for help and immediately begin teaching the lesson she wanted us to learn. Sometimes she just dismissed us: "What did you expect? I told you not to do that."

Recently, I asked my brother if he thinks that our mother loved him. He quickly replied, "I think she probably did, but we were never close. I didn't feel loved or unloved. It was more of a neutral thing. I didn't know what was missing, so I didn't miss it. It wasn't as though something was there and then taken away." He continued, "One thing I could never understand was our lack of communication. Sometimes I felt that a wall existed between us. This started in childhood and was especially true in the teenage years when I felt uncomfortable sharing problems and concerns with her. Eventually I stopped trying—and both of us lost."

He reminded me of one day when our family was together and he told about his oldest son taking him to lunch, just to say, "I love you." This was very important to him, because their relationship had been troubled at times. Then he turned to Mother and Dad and said sincerely, "I want you both to know that I love you, too." What prompted Mother to reply, "You've already told us that"? He never again attempted to bridge the distance between them, although he continued to be a good son until they died.

Nor does my sister remember feeling loved. She does remember often wondering, "Now how can I handle this right? I don't want to upset Mother." She remembers that she learned early not to incur Mother's wrath and that she couldn't relate to her on an intimate basis—"If you don't trust that someone is going to listen to you and care about your feelings, you are not willing to take the risks of communication."

For much of my life I wouldn't have thought of sharing certain things with my mother—my lack of friends and popularity in high school, the breakups with boyfriends, how soon and how deeply I cared for my husband when we began dating, problems during my four pregnancies, the conflicts with my children when they were teenagers, worrisome health situations, or the years I spent in therapy trying to understand why I had so much difficulty with depression. Maybe I didn't want to risk upsetting her. Maybe I didn't want to be told, "It's your own fault."

I feel quite sure that Mother wanted to do what she thought was best for her children. There was much she wanted us to learn. She sacrificed all manner of things so that I could take piano lessons. But I don't remember her ever complimenting my playing even when Daddy sang in public and I accompanied him. She seemed to think it was unbecoming to feel pride in one's accomplishments.

She probably did the best job she could with the tools she was given. She certainly succeeded in instilling an important work ethic in her children. Our values and morals are sharply honed. My brother, my sister, and I often felt guilty for our actions when we were young, but we grew into hard-working adults with a strong sense of integrity.

I will never know why Mother seemed so vulnerable to me, but one of my sons commented when we talked of her, "Children have a deep sensibility about emotional fragility, although it is on an inexpressible and inaccessible level."

And perhaps my daughter summed it up well: "I think the whole family sensed at some level that your mother was fragile—she required special care and feeding—just like her violets."

Perceptions

*W*ould Mother's perceptions of herself have matched ours?

My own four children remember many of the things I did for them—sewing a special party dress in the wee hours of the night, as a surprise for my daughter; helping with homework; taking time to talk about little things as well as big; driving my three sons to mow lawns while they were still too young to drive and crocheting afghans in the car while I waited for them to finish.

They do not remember the batches and batches of cookies I made or the pans of hot cinnamon rolls I served with soup for Saturday suppers. They can point to numerous times when they felt I wasn't there for them (and did so frequently when they were young), but recently when I asked each of them if they had felt loved as children, not one hesitated: "Very much so." I am grateful for that and I am pleased to see how well they parent their own children.

Although my brother, my sister, and I do not remember feeling loved as children, I'm certain our parents would have been shocked to realize we feel that way.

Mother was dismayed when I wrote a piece for my first book about needing to be rocked and held and loved. She couldn't get over my not remembering being hugged as a child. I asked her if she recalled hugs from her childhood. "Of course not!" she huffed.

I asked many of Mother's thirteen grandchildren for their thoughts. Some had perceptions that were significantly different from mine.

Grammie was known for baking Christmas cookies with and for her grandchildren, sewing beautiful doll outfits, stirring up homemade paste and modeling clay, and thinking up all manner of art projects.

Almost all of the grandchildren with whom I talked felt loved by both their parents and their grandparents. They expressed exceptionally fond memories of pleasant and loving times, especially with their grandmother. One said he had had "simply remarkable conversations" with her. Another told of "long, intimate talks." A third mentioned that at times Mother had seemed a bit misleading, but he had always felt that was subconscious, rather than calculated.

Several recalled her less favorably.

One grandson commented, "I had a sense that Grammie loved our 'cuteness' when we were small, and it was fun making gingerbread houses and decorating the Christmas cookies. But as I grew older, I couldn't help feeling that we were somehow responsible for her happiness. The whole thing was an enigma to me—the kindness she showed us contrasted with the bitterness she expressed about her own life and the way she and Poppa bickered right in front of me. Sometimes I felt very uncomfortable."

I was startled to discover that for most of her life, my thirty-five-year-old niece, a counselor who majored in psychology and sociology, felt even more distanced from my mother than we children did. She told me:

> *When circumstances separated me from my own mother at age two, Grandma Sally [her maternal grandmother] stepped in to help out. I formed quite a deep attachment to her. She was my mother. She died when I was a preteen; I was devastated. At that point, Grammie tried to spend more time with me. It was hard for me to respond. There wasn't a lot of access to my heart.*
>
> *I couldn't love her the way she wanted to be loved. That made me feel very bad about myself whenever I*

was around her, so I tried to compensate and be overly nice to her. The more I tried, the more resentful she was. It felt like she was saying, "You had your chance; don't buddy up now."

This continued all through high school and college. As I got older, I couldn't figure out why there was so much distance between us. I almost felt she was just doing her Christian duty with me. It seemed to me that her other two granddaughters connected well with her. Why couldn't I? I kept thinking, "This is Grammie *and everybody loves her. What is the matter with* me?*"*

After I graduated from college, I thought perhaps our relationship would go better because I'd chosen a helping profession—and sometimes it seemed as if it did.

But when my husband and I rented a house less than a block away from hers, the situation got really yucky for me. I was a new mother, trying to understand my role and my feelings.

For awhile, I tried to visit Grammie every other Sunday and I thought she was proud of me, but it always seemed that she wanted more, that she was saying, "You came this Sunday, but where were you last Sunday?"

I went less and less often, because every time I visited, I felt worse about myself. It was as if I'd done something to wound her, but she wouldn't tell me what it was. Whenever I tried to talk to her, she became silent and distant. I was desperate. I called myself a helper and I couldn't even reach my own grandmother.

After we decided to move away from the city, I finally phoned her: "I know you're upset with me. I didn't mean to upset you. May I spend some time with you before we go?"

She replied, "You've lived here two years and you haven't spent time with me. Why would you want to see me now?" I told her I would at least like to come to say good-bye. She said, "I would prefer you didn't," and hung up.

The only time I saw her after that was when I flew to Denver to visit her just before she died. I told her once again how sorry I was about how I had treated her. She replied, "It's okay. I forgive you for everything. It will be all right."

My theory is that the people who could see that she shut down sometimes, those who could sense her sadness, are the ones from whom she moved away. She was comfortable with those who saw her as Grandmother; she was good in that role.

Were the other grandchildren insulated in some way that this one wasn't? Without that insulation, was she simply treated as one of the children?

Another granddaughter felt she had a good relationship with Mother, from which she derived a lot of happiness and received much encouragement. But she also felt the sadness and at times felt inadequate in her grandmother's eyes.

Mother's friends dearly loved her. She nurtured them well, consistently remembering birthdays, anniversaries, and deaths. One of her closest friends told me that Mother was always very kind and interested in what she was doing and what was going on in her life.

She added, "I was so impressed with the way she kept putting energy into being open to change, to being non-judgmental, to being positive, even when she had to sort out difficult things like divorce in light of her background and what she had been taught." When this friend took another woman as her life partner in the 1980s, Mother accepted them without reservation.

As I have talked with others, it has become clearer and clearer that my mother was a complex woman who meant different things to different people.

Perception is not the same as reality—nevertheless, we cannot change how it felt for us.

The Butter Churn

I remember churning white cream in the old glass churn with the wooden paddle and the gray metal daisy wheel.

Grandma was right beside me, directing every move, making sure I knew when to stop, chatting with me as if I were a grownup—about everything and nothing—as we watched the cream slowly turn into pale yellow butter. I don't know if Grandma liked churning butter when I wasn't there, but clearly she loved being with me.

Grandma died suddenly one fine August morning, when I was almost twenty-one—just six weeks before my first child was born two months prematurely—without so much as a good-bye or a backward look.

Her meager belongings were packed up and brought to my mother's house to be divided among Grandma's six children. I'm not sure whether Mother chose the butter churn or whether it was just left behind, but it ended up at her house, stashed in the back of the pantry under the stairs.

Over the years, from time to time, I would ask her if I could have it. It wasn't as though it was making butter or even decorating the house. She always said, "No."

Many years later, when I lived in my third house and had traded the Danish Modern phase for Early American, I begged Mother, "Please let me have the churn. I'm the only one who can remember making butter with Grandma."

Once again she said, "No. It wouldn't be fair to your sister or brother. Why do you want something so old, anyway? Besides, it wouldn't look right in your house." My sister didn't want the butter churn and my brother didn't even know it existed.

But when Mother's strength for keeping everything tidy began to wane, she began to lighten the load of her possessions. She offered things she no longer wanted to the three of us—milk glass party plates, delicate bone china teacups, several pieces of Roseville pottery, her glass punch bowl. . . .

Grandma's old butter churn sits on my counter now. It looks fine. It fills the kitchen with love.

"The Old Butter Churn"

Photo by Lois Tschetter Hjelmstad

In Spite of Everything

I have coped all my years
with her flaws
     her negativity
     her manipulations
     her holding us at bay

I have relied all my years
on her strengths
     unswerving loyalty
     commitment to "getting it right"
     a strong work ethic
     unwavering faith
     beauty in every endeavor

In spite of either—or both—
I have always loved her

The author with her parents

How Can I Love Her?

It isn't as though we had no warning.

It isn't as though cancer has been a stranger in my life. I have had two mastectomies and have written a book about my experience titled *Fine Black Lines: Reflections on Facing Cancer, Fear and Loneliness.* I travel around the country, even to foreign countries, speaking to various groups about cancer.

But somehow it comes like a bolt out of the blue. I had no premonition, even though Mother's knee has been sore for a number of weeks and it seems to be getting worse.

The Christmas season was lovely. Mother and Dad were with Les, our children, and me on Christmas Eve; had Christmas brunch with my sister, Jan, and her family; and enjoyed Christmas dinner with my brother, Nick, and his family. Everyone had a wonderful time.

After Christmas dinner, Dad and Nick went to Nick's mountain house, so Mother was home alone when she experienced severe pain in her bad knee in the wee hours of the night. When Dad returned the next day, she explained that she had done nothing at the time except suffer, because she hadn't known whom to call. *Didn't know whom to call? I live only two miles away.*

December 27—The knee is x-rayed. There is a tumor on her fibula.

December 28—Mother calls to say they will remove the tumor tomorrow. It dawns on me that she could have bone cancer and it may have come from her breast. When I was first diagnosed with breast cancer, I suggested she get a mammogram, because my diagnosis put her at higher risk, but she refused.

December 29—Les and I pick up Mom and Dad at 5:15 a.m. and take them to the hospital. We sit and wait until noon for her biopsy. We won't know the results until tomorrow, but the doctors seem somewhat encouraged.

December 30—Mom's diagnosis is metastatic adenocarcinoma. The doctors don't know where it originated. While Jan, Nick, and I debate how, when, and if to tell Mother that she has cancer, her doctor calls to tell her the tumor is malignant. Les and I stop by to see Mom and Dad. He is devastated. She is uncharacteristically cheerful. I'm numb.

Is she in denial, or doesn't she care if she dies?

December 31—Dad says he isn't going to say anything to anyone yet, because "although it is assumed to be cancer, we don't really know much." Mother has a CT scan. The doctor tells Nick [who is also a physician] that the primary site is her lung and it could well be terminal in less than two years.

January 1—Nick, Jan, and I have talked for hours. Yesterday, we discussed whether or not we should tell Mother about the lung cancer and its untenable prognosis, and urge her to halt unnecessary tests and treatment, but we abandoned that plan. We cannot make decisions for her. It is her right to decide.

Her bone scan is Monday; the doctor will then tell her what we already know and offer options. We'll have a sibling meeting on January 5th to deal with our feelings, so we can come to agreement and present a united front, if possible.

Dad is very upset because Mom told her sister today that she would not do chemotherapy. He thinks he has a say. This loss of control is hard for him. He is frantic that he will lose her. It is coming as a distinct shock to him that the era of men making the decisions for women may be over.

Our concern is that she truly understands what she's deciding, without letting the power issues she has with Dad cloud her judgment.

I remember how difficult it was when I was diagnosed with breast cancer five years ago. Life is spinning out of control again with Mom's diagnosis of cancer.

I think we have a very rocky road ahead.

January 2—I need to define myself so I know who I am. I need to find the high road and then commit to walking it.

January 4—I couldn't sleep last night and had to breathe into a brown bag because I was hyperventilating. My blood pressure hit 190/100 today. I do not normally have high blood pressure.

My parents call to say they have good news. The lung thing is a calcium deposit that has been there a long time. The leg thing is an infection. The leg thing is an _infection_? Denial is an amazing coping mechanism.

January 5—Nick, Renée [his wife], Jan, and Fred [her husband] join Les and me for dinner. We commiserate.

We've been thinking it would be best to gently remind Mom and Dad of the realities, but perhaps it doesn't matter. They need to handle it whatever way they can.

When I was diagnosed with breast cancer, I wanted as much information as possible. That does not mean they do.

We discuss how we can best provide our parents with whatever they need. The closeness we feel warms our cold hearts.

January 12—I try to talk with Mother and Dad about the ramifications of the radiation therapy she's been offered—the burden of going for daily treatments, additional fatigue, and possible burns. Since I had weeks of radiation therapy myself, I feel I can add a perspective that the medical people are less likely to offer.

They become angry when I answer questions they have not yet asked.

Dad interrupts me. "Lois, you're very sincere and I know you mean well. You've written a book about your experience and it's important to you. What really bothers me, Lois, is that you scare people with your knowledge. You're not doing a service to some people by sharing your experience. You're not a doctor."

Obviously, as far as they are concerned, I have overstepped the boundaries of involvement. Perhaps I am only revisiting my own decisions. Mother's cancer has brought up old feelings about my cancer as well as a deep fear of losing her, and regret, always regret.

I am sixty-four years old and they are eighty-seven, but I feel like a small, reprimanded child. They insist they know more about this than I do. I only meant to enlighten them, but I've upset them instead.

Their discounting my experience hurts and overwhelms me. I can't provide support when I feel rejected. It is like getting an electric shock each time you try to hug someone—an old pattern that doesn't change.

Perhaps their dignity and need for control do not allow them to be "mothered" by their daughter. If I had just waited until they asked how radiation had been for me, I might have said, "I've been there. This will not be easy. What are you hoping the outcome will be?"

I could have remembered that honesty does not require that we tell all we know—only that we tell no untruth.

January 14—I call to ask how it is going. Dad says, "The initial shock was terrible. The first twenty-four hours I felt bewildered, but now we're making progress in a direction that meets my needs."

Mom says, "I'm not as alarmed as Dad is. I'm thankful it isn't in my colon and that I'm as old as I am."

They are going ahead with the radiation.

Ambivalence

How can I hate her—

> frail, delicate woman
> beautiful of face and spirit
> giver of my life
> giving to others
> facing painful death
> without complaint

How can I love her—

> frightening me with her dying
> turning my life upside down
> seeming not to know or care
> how much she is hurting me

On a Shared Diagnosis

*W*hen I was diagnosed with breast cancer, I waited almost two weeks before I told my parents. I could not bear to shatter their illusions that I would always be there for them.

Finally, the morning before my first mastectomy, I reluctantly drove to their house.

It was worse than I had expected. Mother's face froze in shock. Dad's stooped shoulders slumped even more. We sat in silence. Then, desperately, I tried to cheer them with pledges and promises, saying anything to breathe life into Mother's still expression and to get Dad to lift his shoulders.

I will be fine—don't worry
I wouldn't think of dying
Be reassured, my loves

I had no right to promise. There is no way to know.

Months later, when writing *Fine Black Lines*, I realized that although I might imagine how I would feel if my daughter told me such a thing, I really had no clue to how they felt about my diagnosis and treatment. It was presumptuous of me to think I could know what they experienced. So I asked them if they would write a page describing their immediate reactions. They were taken aback. Mother exclaimed, "Oh, my!" Dad said he didn't need to make a list—he could summarize it all with one word: "Horrible."

It was clear they did not want to think about my situation any more than absolutely necessary. They needed time to process.

It was two years after that conversation when Mother gave me the following note for my birthday:

> *You've asked me to write how I felt when you told us*
> *you had cancer. As you know, or remember, I simply*
> *froze. The shock was so great I could neither speak nor*
> *cry. Thoughts of all the times we've spent together*
> *came to mind—our shopping trips, Friday lunches,*
> *holidays at your house and ours. Then I was grateful*
> *that we had all this time together, but very sad that*
> *maybe it would never be again. As time wore on, it*
> *became apparent to me that this was real and I must*
> *deal with it.*
>
> *I believe that no matter what happens to any of us in*
> *the future, we will have the strength to face it.*

Much as that note comforted me, Mother basically stayed in denial about my breast cancer just as she later denied her lung cancer. I felt that I had something to offer, but she became contentious whenever I tried to make a connection through our mutual fight against cancer. Perhaps she was too frightened to deal with death. Perhaps I was too much like my father.

Mother and I shared many things throughout our lives. Our common diagnosis was not to be one of them.

Cancer

Mother, I would fold you
close to my breasts—
except I don't have any. . .

And now the disease
that flattened my chest

is choking the very breath
from your body. . .

January 21—I walk to Friday lunch with Mom and Dad. Jan is there, too, and as we discuss the sixty-fifth wedding anniversary coming up in June, we discover Dad has already talked to our pastor and has everything planned out.

Jan brings me home. She says she is troubled by how antagonistic Mother is to me.

February 18—I have a good conversation with Mom and Dad at lunch, but it hurts to see them so old and so far down the road to termination. At least the radiation treatments are finished.

February 25—I observe that they are really struggling—physically, emotionally. It will be helpful if they can, even at this late date, learn to give more support to one another, rather than continue their lifelong scramble for power and control.

February 27—Mom and Dad come for dinner and we have a fairly pleasant evening until she once again starts talking negatively about the past, about her life. It is sad to realize how little Mother can accept reality as she lived it. I cannot imagine someone regretting a life as much as she does. Perhaps she is asking for reassurance that she has been a good mother and has lived a worthwhile life.

I wish that my parents could openly express disagreements and disappointments so they could resolve them and clear the air. Sometimes I feel I have spent a lifetime dodging their barbs and breathing hostilities; however, it is their marriage. They bring to it what they have.

April 3—Is there any chance that Mother will be alive next Easter?

April 8—Mother looks pale and fragile. I try to talk with her about how she feels. She doesn't want to discuss her health or her psyche.

April 29—Lunch is an intense experience. Dad says that he has figured out why they fight so much. His mother had not treated my mother well and he thinks that has affected how Mother feels about him. Sometimes I wonder if Mom's feelings about Dad are why she disliked his mother so.

Right after they were married, Dad took Mother home to the family farm, where he worked throughout that summer, prior to returning to teaching in the fall. It was difficult for my delicate, refined mother to live with his rough-hewn family—especially the first summer she was married. It was probably hard for them, too, since my grandmother had picked out a different mate for her son. Somehow it set a bad tone for their marriage. I'm not sure they have ever overcome the feelings generated that summer.

May 8—I invite Mom and Dad to share a casserole and gelatin salad to celebrate Mother's Day. I give her embroidered dishtowels plus a pretty necklace and earrings. She seems pleased. Les and I talk about some of the good experiences we have had through our travels with *Fine Black Lines*. For a little while, I feel connected. I wonder if this could be her last Mother's Day.

May 17—We take the folks to the airport. They are flying to South Dakota to attend Dad's seventieth high school reunion. They seem frail, but pleased to be going. I'm glad that Mother is doing things she wouldn't have made the effort to do before.

She has spent her life being careful and admonishing others to do the same. I don't know whether she lost her spirit of adventure somewhere along the way or whether she was born without a sense that life is something to be treasured and embraced, even at some risk.

Mother has protected herself well throughout her life—physically and emotionally.

Gossamer

Life is a thread
    delicate, iridescent, fragile,
    a tenuous strand
    an intricate design

tying the spirit
to its body

floating gently on the breeze
swaying as the winds rise
stretching in the gale

Love this world as long
as the gossamer shall hold—

one day
that strand will break
and free the spirit

to soar toward
a new dimension

The Seasons Pass

*M*other continued to steadfastly deny her diagnosis. Although she would admit to having had a "little problem" with her knee, she insisted the surgery and radiation had fixed it. Even though her whole family knew better, her insistence lulled us into the hope that she might live forever. For fourteen months, we stayed in denial.

Mother and Dad celebrated their sixty-fifth wedding anniversary that June. She said later that all the beautiful flowers and heartfelt comments made her feel as if she were attending her own funeral.

She often complained about being very tired, but she always had. In September, she bought four pairs of pretty pajamas.

At Christmas, she had a very sore shoulder, which she treated with aspirin and a heating pad. She joined Dad in the round of festivities in a spirit of determined good cheer.

Was stoicism as much an accomplishment for Mother's generation as being able to "express ourselves" is for ours? Did they accept troubles and dying more readily? Did they have a sense of reality that our generation doesn't because we've been told over and over that life should always be good?

In February, a year after Mother's initial treatment, our attempt at denial was shattered. I have no way of knowing how long Mother was able to continue hers.

Wedding of the author's parents

I Go into the Kitchen and Weep

February 20—In the midst of a struggle to get *Fine Black Lines* reprinted, I'm having another axillary dissection day after tomorrow to determine whether the new lump under my arm is cancerous. Mother is going to the doctor today about her backache. Yesterday, Bob [my oldest son] gave me an outdated computer from his office. I need it desperately, but I've never touched a computer before. Help!

February 23—It is a very good news/very bad news day. My biopsy appears to be okay, but Mother's doctor tells Nick that the bone scan she had yesterday showed cancer in her spine, pelvis, and ribs, as well as her lungs.

February 24—Dad takes Mother in to talk about her tests. The doctor thinks she looks so ill and fragile that he hospitalizes her. Fred [Jan's husband, who is a cardiologist] tells Dad about the bone scan results. Dad looks stunned. We are all stunned, even though we've known she's had lung cancer since a year ago Christmas.

February 25—Dad calls to report that the oncologist says Mom has three to six months to live. Nick also talks to the oncologist, who tells him it will probably be closer to three months. The doctor suggests to Nick that Mother got the cancer from Dad's smoking. Since he quit over fifty years ago, I find that difficult to believe, but I was exposed to the same risk. That's scary.

Dad asks for a family meeting, so I invite him for dinner, together with Jan and Fred, and Nick and Renée. It is very sad to have a family gathering without Mother. I cry for a long time after they leave, but planning for her care when she comes home from the hospital and sharing our feelings is helpful.

February 26—I had trouble sleeping after last night's emotional evening. I walk after lunch and then try to rest, but Dad drops by to report that Mom will stay in intermediate care during the three weeks she has radiation. He is almost euphoric and she seems to be absolutely delighted. What can I say?

They have discussed hospice, too, as I suggested.

February 27—The phone calls begin early. The situation changes from minute to minute. Now Mom is coming home tomorrow after Dad goes to Lions Club. I notice that frantic phone calls back and forth are a coping mechanism. It works for me.

February 28—I talk to Mom at great length, trying to reassure her. She is not coming home today after all.

March 1—I am extremely tired. My chronic fatigue syndrome [which I contracted before I had breast cancer] does not respond well to stress. I ache from head to toe; the lymph nodes in my neck are swollen; I have difficulty concentrating. The medicine I take for osteoporosis makes me feel even sicker.

In contrast, my piano teaching is especially meaningful. The students play well. I can see that they care about the piano and their music more than I have realized, even those I imagine to be least interested. Children are so clear and so deep.

When we go to see Mom, I ask how she is. "Fine," she snaps. She is lying there, whiter than the sheets, so I insist, "No, how are you really?" She retorts, "What's the matter? Do you want me to be sick? Do you want me to be like you?"

Very little upsets Les, but Mom's caustic answers do. He tells me later that he almost whisked me from the room to take me home.

It is only by trying to see the small, frightened child within Mother that I can deal with such incidents.

Both of my parents are eldest children and I am their oldest child. Consequently, I knew all four of my grandparents quite well for many years. My mother's childhood was not easy. She has lived much of her life as an irritable woman, as did her mother. Why would she not be cranky under the present circumstances? Why would she not be angry at being forced to relinquish the coping mechanism of denial that has worked for more than a year?

I have wondered if chronic low-grade depression is genetic in our family. Would medication or learning to understand her feelings help her be more comfortable in her body?

No matter what the reason, I feel very sad about how she treats me. I wish she could be more open. I hope we can grieve this death together.

My body is shutting down and my spirit is, too.

Yesterday when Jan visited the hospital, Mom and Dad fought so much about so many little things that she finally just told them she was leaving and walked out.

Sometimes I think there is a fantasy, widely held, that adversity brings people closer—that trouble heals old wounds and sets the stage for new harmony. To some extent, and in some families, this may be true.

But in my life, crisis puts everyone on edge and exacerbates the difficulties. It crystallizes existing problems. There are a dozen opinions about what should be done. We hold many phone conversations filled with "he said," "she said." Often, we distance ourselves—physically, emotionally, and sometimes even spiritually.

Yes, there is a fantasy. It is held mainly by those who have not experienced much adversity.

Time Out

This time
I flee
the fray

And sit here in peace
my heart quietly

b
  r   e   a   k   i   n   g

March 2—I roll out of bed and onto my computer chair. I work until noon, revising a letter to my printing company, explaining why I am dissatisfied with their work. Just as I get the letter the way I want it, I accidentally delete it.

Then I drive to the clinic to have the stitches from the biopsy removed. Driving makes my arm ache, but the final pathology report on my biopsy confirms the good news. *Whew!*

March 3—Mom comes home. Dad and I have another discussion about his primary responsibility to Mom. He simply announces, "I will not give up Lions Club or my club projects. If I have to give up any of my activities, you may as well bury me, too."

I wonder if this is not only a symptom of his denial, but part of an unconscious drive to maintain his own life. Maybe he knows intuitively that he will need to have a life waiting for him when Mom is gone. Maybe it provides respite from the pain and pressure of watching her suffer.

Dad called Jan one day recently and stated, "I am going to Lions Club today. Get with your brother and sister and see who is coming to take care of Mother."

At first he was quite angry that we are setting limits. He feels we are shirking our duty. After much discussion, I think he understands that we do support him.

It is another power struggle. If he can't get his three children to do what he wants, how he wants it, and when he wants it, he interprets our independence as a lack of interest.

We maintain a delicate balance between pushing him to keep his marital commitment (for his sake as much as for hers) and remembering that it is also *our* best and last chance to do something for Mother.

I finally connect with Mother. I wonder if it is as important for her as it is for me? We grieve some together. She tells me that she is going ahead to make things ready for the rest of us. That's what you have always done, Mom. *That's what you have always done.*

If the end should come before I have another chance, I will feel I have properly said good-bye. But—God, I hate to lose her.

March 4—Les drops me off at the house. Mom and Dad seem more settled into the situation. They have an appointment to talk to the home hospice organization this coming Monday at 1:00. Mother is steadily losing ground. She becomes weaker and paler each day.

I walk home on the bike path through Harvard Gulch. My thoughts are long and deep. How can I leave for the Phoenix book tour next week? What is *my* commitment and responsibility in this crisis?

March 5—Mother seems better. She has more color and her voice is stronger.

When I mention my upcoming speaking tour, Mom wonders if I haven't done enough already. She has never understood why I spent so much time writing *Fine Black Lines* in the first place. My ongoing travel and speaking engagements escape her completely. I know she would much rather I stay here with her. For someone who has done as much for others as she has, it seems odd she doesn't understand my desire to bring comfort to other breast cancer patients and survivors.

Later she asks Fred if he doesn't think I've done enough. He replies, "She's doing a lot of good. What is enough?" *Bless him.*

March 6—I set up my students' Group I recital table early. Dad calls at 8:30. Mother feels shaky. She forgot her dose of morphine last night, so she took it this morning. She wants to return to the hospital, because she has a radiation treatment scheduled and can't imagine getting there and back in the snow and cold.

We hurry over. Les carries her to the car, and we take them to the hospital. I feel upset that we have come within four hours of getting hospice set up. If it had been in place, this hospitalization would not be occurring.

This recital is not one of the best, but I'm so tired and distracted that I probably wouldn't recognize a good one.

March 7—Mother says, "I feel dreadful. I just want to die. All I ask is that I be made comfortable."

First there is going to be a meeting with her doctor tomorrow, then there isn't, then there is. The recital this evening for Group II is great. Maybe I *can* tell the difference.

March 8—A big negotiation session with the printer resolves our differences.

Freed from that major pressure, we dash to the hospital to say good-bye to Mother until we return from the book tour. She is staying in the extended care unit for the rest of her radiation therapy as originally planned. She refuses to go home. I think she feels safer in the hospital. She also comments that she loves all the attention.

Tonight's Group III recital is wonderful, but having a hose break and flood the basement afterward is not. We finally get everything cleaned up. We load the car and drive to Las Vegas, New Mexico. We arrive at midnight.

March 11—The tour is going well. I call home again. Mother seems more like herself. I feel better about being gone knowing she will be well cared for in the hospital. Dad feels good about all the arrangements made with home hospice for when she is released.

On the phone, Nick comments that he senses I will feel both guilty and devastated in the end. *Oh, thanks a lot, Nick.* I guess I don't want to be enlightened any more than Mom and Dad did about radiation.

March 13—I call Mother again. She seems almost giddy as she chats and giggles. My mother is the only person I have ever known who actually says "Tee, hee!" when she laughs. Everything has been worked out for her to come home on Friday into hospice care. We will be back in town on Saturday.

March 16—Mom asks Dad if he's made arrangements for her to have twenty-four-hour nursing. Even though she is accustomed to the round-the-clock care, he plans to care for her himself. There will be an aide from hospice for two hours each day, and of course, the rest of us will help.

Dad is bringing her home tomorrow and then leaving for the Men's Retreat an hour later. One of Mother's close friends is coming to stay with her for the weekend. *Should this upset me?*

March 18—We go to see Mother as soon as we get back in town. I am relieved to be home so I can watch over her. She did come home yesterday and Dad did go to the Men's Retreat.

Maybe it was best after all that she settled in on her own with her friend. Perhaps that was why she encouraged Dad to go ahead with his plans.

As passionate as I have been about getting Mom into the hospice program, the reality of that hospital bed in the dining room chills my heart.

Am I afraid that the presence of hospice is not only heralding the end, but somehow hastening it? Is this why people often wait to call hospice until they have missed much of the comfort and courage that is available?

Obviously, a cure is out of the question, so it makes sense to concentrate on Mom's comfort and quality of life, and on coming to terms with its cessation. Now that the time for heroics is over, has the time for contemplation begun?

Admitting the inevitability of her death is profoundly difficult for me. Fear of the death of our mothers stalks us throughout life. To see it happening to mine appalls me.

March 20—I had not planned to visit Mother today until Karen [my daughter] calls to say that Mother's chest is heaving a lot. I go to check.

It takes my seven-year-old granddaughter to say it best: "Doesn't Grammie know she is 'heart-breaking' us?"

March 21—I am over at the house when the regular hospice nurse comes to check Mother for the first time. Joy thinks the breathing difficulties are the result of the right lung having a very limited capacity. I can see Mom dying and I'm not ready. *Wait for me, Mom! Wait for me.*

I have no rest before I begin the evening's long piano teaching schedule. My body is exhausted; my mind is exhausted; my heart is exhausted.

March 22—I have been thinking of writing a poem for Mom, but have procrastinated. After the morning lessons, I feel even more urgency. I go into my office, close the door, and begin to write. In two hours of solitude I compose my farewell.

I take the poem to Mother. She tries to read it, but her arms begin to shake and she struggles to breathe. When I finish reading it to her, she reaches for a tissue, puts it over her face, and just sobs. All she can say is, "Thank you." It is all I need.

Farewell, Beloved Mother

What can I say to you, beloved mother,
as you embark on your last journey?

What can I say to you, beautiful friend,
as I watch you leave my horizon?

What can I say to you
as I see your fragile body growing
ever more fragile and shutting down?

Shall I tell you of memories, of minutia?

> rocking in your arms by the pot-bellied
> stove
> slender hands stitching my wedding dress
> your paintings adorning my walls
> grandmothering raised to an art form
> sunny afternoons of talk and silence
> shopping trips, finding just what you
> wanted
> impeccable grooming, gracious inner
> beauty
> your sweet smile as you listened at
> recitals

Shall I tell you of my gratitudes?

> gift of life from your small body
> skills and zest for homemaking
> encouragement for my teaching
> confidences shared and guarded

What can I say to you, dearest mother
as I see you abandon this dimension?

You have always been beautiful—
you are more beautiful now
you have always been courageous—
you are most courageous now

What can I wish for you, cherished mother,
as you reach toward the new tomorrow?

> I trust your journey will be safe
> I pray your journey will be peaceful
> I know your reward is secure

I have always loved you
I will miss you forever

Farewell, beloved mother
Farewell, beloved friend

March 23—Mom's heart rate is 140. Joy wants her to use the oxygen continuously because her heart has to work too hard to get the oxygen where it needs to go.

Since Mother has been sleeping a great deal the past few days, Joy reduces the dosage of the pain medication. She explains that since the radiation therapy has relieved much of Mom's pain, the amount of narcotics she has been taking is overdosing her. Pain is an antidote for narcotics. When Mother was having a lot of pain, she was not oversedated, but now she is.

Mother's only sister is planning to come on April 10. I'm afraid it will be too late. *Too late.*

March 24—Jan and I meet Joy at the house. Joy insists that Mother stay on the oxygen. It now appears that she may actually get better for awhile. Perhaps, with portable oxygen, she can even get out a bit. The doctor sees no reason why she can't be up, doing things around the house. My hopes are high for her coming to our traditional Easter dinner. This is an emotional roller coaster.

Joy tells us that when people face the terminal reality, there's a shift in their thinking. Then, if they have reached readiness but don't die, they feel inconvenienced by living with a handicap—in this case, breathing problems and oxygen. They are not prepared to live with incapacitation. The question becomes, "Now what do I do?"

Vignette

> Helplessly I watch
> as they make their mad dash
> to the bathroom
>> her pale, thin arm clutching his
>> their weary feet shuffling
>> over the light Berber carpet
>> their bodies stooped with
>> the weight of many years
>
> They've been together since
> they were very young
> sometimes they've been happy
> sometimes life's been up, sometimes not
> but here they walk side by side
>> as cancer interrupts
>> whatever they were doing
>> as cancer eats her body
>> and tears his heart
>
> "In sickness and in health," they vowed
> "until death do us part," they vowed
>
> Helplessly I watch
> and then
> I go into the kitchen and weep. . .

"Communion"

Photo by Connie Rempel

A Loaf of Bread, A Cup of Wine

March 27—Joy brings the digitalis the doctor ordered because Mother's heart rate is still high, even with continual oxygen. Joy takes a blood sample because Mother is not only somewhat jaundiced, but she is still too sleepy.

When I am alone with Mother, she questions, "Do I have cancer?" I wonder why she asks. She says that her internist indicated that she'd be around for awhile, and that her oncologist has dismissed her from his care.

She lowers her voice a bit and confides, "I don't think I have cancer."

I don't know if she is confused or if suddenly she is very clear in a way I can't comprehend. How can she possibly not know she has cancer?

March 28—When I get to the house today, Dad says, "Take off your coat and feed your mother." Apparently she won't eat. Joy says that she really doesn't have to eat if she doesn't want to. Eating is very tedious for someone who is short of breath.

I think Dad so badly wants her to live that he takes her lack of appetite as a personal affront. He looks a bit ragged.

March 29—Joy calls to say that the lab tests show some problems with Mom's liver, which may be contributing to her anorexia, confusion, lack of energy, and sleepiness. We don't know if it is another metastasis or an acute problem. It is not good news.

I walk home in an extraordinarily beautiful spring snow. I am amazed to see so much beauty at such a sad time. Spring is breaking my heart.

March 30—Mother appears more jaundiced today. As usual, she has several visitors, some of whom overstay a bit. I wish they would call first to see if their visits are convenient. I end up having no time alone with her. I find this very distressing. I feel others are taking away time I could be spending with my mother. I am aware of trying to form a deeper bond, even in these last days.

March 31—Joy thinks the jaundice is improved. Dad goes to the grocery store while I am here, so I have a few minutes alone with Mother. While I warm her hands in mine, we have a good talk. Such moments calm my heart.

Universe

One spring evening I walk
    overwhelmed
    in body, in spirit
    in situation beyond my control

In a moment of utter despair
I fling myself to
the slightly damp ground

As I beseech
the immense twilight dome
I suddenly feel relevant

I am a link—
I am a link between
the Earth and the Sky

And just as suddenly
I know, I absolutely know
that I can do
    whatever I need to do
    however long I need to do it

It is an incredible enlightenment
It is an amazing assessment
It is a consoling concept

April 1—Mother sleeps part of the two hours I visit, but we have a good hour together. Her breathing seems labored and she is wheezing. I feel despondent today. My spirits are usually steady, but I've been working hard and I'm very upset about Mother. I am just so *tired*.

April 2—I am in the tub when Dad calls to report that the nurse on call will be there in less than fifteen minutes. I dash over to the house.

The breathing and wheezing are worse. I'm glad I am there as the nurse gives new instructions. Knowing help is available around the clock is comforting. At noon Les brings fast food and we have lunch with Mom and Dad. She barely touches her hamburger and favorite strawberry shake.

April 3—Joy is already at the house when I arrive. Since Mother had choked on some food last Saturday afternoon, we discuss when it might be appropriate to call 911. Mother has requested no heroic measures. Joy says that choking might be the only time we should call 911. She promises to make sure the doctor has signed the DNR [Do Not Resuscitate].

Mother and I are also concerned that her breathing will just get harder and harder until she suffocates. Joy reassures us, explaining that there is a way to administer morphine that allows patients to feel comfortable even though they are not getting enough air. Mother seems as relieved as I am.

I am proud of Dad. I ask him what his best-case scenario would be. He replies, "I want to keep her at home. I want to care for her myself, no matter how messy it gets. I'd rather clean up diarrhea than subject her to the indignity of wearing a diaper. I want to fulfill my marriage vow of 'in sickness and in health, until death do us part.' I wish I could have her in my bed and hold her."

I can sense how desperately he wants her to be the way she had been. When he says he wants to hold her in his arms once again, I suggest that he simply lift her over and crawl into the hospital bed beside her.

I wonder if he will.

April 4—Mom and Dad want their family to come for a communion and anointing service, so we gather at their home tonight. Our pastors bring the necessary items and perform the familiar service. All of us—parents, children, and mates—are able to express our feelings, our appreciation, and our love for Mother, as well as give support to one another. It is the most moving event I have ever experienced with my original family.

It is a comfort, even as my heart is filled with sadness, to confront death once again and to see it is not the enemy.

Maybe there isn't an enemy. . .

Last Communion

We had planned the event hurriedly—
with little concern we'd be too soon
and much concern we'd be too late.

A fresh bouquet of spring flowers
graced the coffee table.
Mother's hospital stand
became an altar with
a linen cloth, a wooden cross,
a loaf of bread, a cup of wine.

Mother sat, swallowed by her chair,
her face pale and wan,
her hair a frame of silver.

The oxygen concentrator belched
in a corner, drowning out
the gentle sighs. The mechanical bed
lurked in the shadows
of the dining room.

We broke the bread and
drank the wine,
told the stories of love
and whispered our good-byes—
one by one. . .

We sat in a circle
that reminded of circles
formed years ago
to open Christmas gifts—
this time we opened our grief.

She smiled and said
it was the best party
she'd ever had.

She cried, but said
she was not afraid.

Quietly, we left the house.

Resolutely she turned to
face her death. . .

Sadly we turned
to face our lives. . .

April 8—Several days ago, Mother gave her painting materials to Bob [my oldest son]. He had expressed an interest in painting at various times, and when he visited, she said she would give him her equipment on the condition that he paint a picture and bring it to her in a week.

Bob is overwhelmed with work. April is not a good month for a tax accountant. But he promised. After working at the office for more than twelve hours, he goes home, puts on a painting video and paints and paints until he finishes his first-ever picture. When it is dry, Mother will get her wish.

April 12—Les and I meet Dad at Hampden Memorial Gardens. He is purchasing a shelf in the mausoleum for Mother's ashes and for—someday—his. It's expensive, but he insists that having their ashes in a geographical location instead of scattering them will assure they are not forgotten.

How can he possibly think we might forget them? If I were deciding, I would certainly opt for the outdoor garden location or just do the cremation as Mother requested and let it go at that. But it's his call.

Mother has a lot of company today. Finally, I simply ask for a private word with her. She cries and asks me why it takes so long to die. Her body has let her down.

April 13—I meet Dad at the mortuary again. He signs the contract. He accuses me of wanting a simpler burial in order to make his estate bigger for us. I can't believe my ears.

Mother calls Karen and asks her to please return the knitting and crocheting materials she had earlier bequeathed her.

April 15—Mother is very alert and doesn't sleep as much today. Her sister is here now, and she helps Mother clean out the sewing drawers as they quietly weep together.

When I was diagnosed with breast cancer five Aprils ago, I remember cleaning my closets and drawers in an effort to simplify my life. I see Mother drawing on that same resource to create order during chaos, to find comfort where there is none. Maybe she is tying up the loose ends of her life as well as her sewing.

He Is Arisen

It is Easter Sunday morning.
I have been preparing
the traditional Easter brunch.
The table is set—
>   beautiful bouquet from the children
>   Old Curiosity Shop plates
>   ruby red glasses sparkling
>   in the glow of the pewter chandelier.

I love to prepare for company.
But I had counted on my mother
being here one last Easter.
My heart is breaking
because she cannot come.
She is tethered to the oxygen tank.
She is constricted by her weakness
and her dying.

I wonder what I am doing
having dinner here with my generation
and my children and my grandchildren.

I do not feel like going on—
I feel like going back.
I want my mother
I need my mother
in the most elemental way.
I need to be a child again.
I need hugs, the warmth of her body,
the faint smell of wild roses.

I need to feel that everything is okay
even though it never really was.

The author's mother, while in college

As If We
Could Forget

April 16—Russ [my youngest son], has left his family back in Michigan to come visit Mother for the last time. Earlier, I had suggested to Keith [my middle son] that maybe he should come, too, but he and his family visited from Illinois at Christmas and he prefers to remember her the way she was then—sitting in her favorite chair, bustling to bring out beverages and Christmas goodies.

When I stop to see her in the afternoon, she gives me some of her sewing materials. Dad just comes unglued.

"You can't give those things away. Legally they are all mine!" he shouts.

"They are my things. I can give them to whomever I wish," she insists.

As I try to be supportive of each of them, I remember the many times over the years that I have felt caught in the middle of their disagreements. Obviously, they feel strongly—Mother in her need to express her connection to me, and Dad in his need to stay the hand of death.

I reassure Mom that I accept what she is giving with gratitude. I attempt to help Dad see that in trying to mask the enormity of how horrendous it all really is, he is getting upset about things that don't matter. How important can a pair of scissors and a set of crochet hooks be to his future? He listens and I hold him as he sobs. I'm not sure I have ever seen him cry before.

I am approaching the limits of my physical body—to say nothing of my mind and especially my heart. There is more than enough pain to go around.

April 17—At my cancer support group tonight, I talk about the deepening chasm I sense between Mom and Dad. I still feel responsible somehow to bring them closer. The other members help me see that it is not my problem. I cannot fill in the gaps. I can't change (nor should I) my parents' coping mechanisms. I need to just let it all go.

So I choose not to referee anymore. I wonder why I tried to for so many years. It has only brought me anguish.

It is amazing how the dying process brings up the unresolved issues of living.

April 20—It is five years since my cancer diagnosis. It is hard to imagine it has been that long; on the other hand, it seems as if I've dealt with cancer my entire life.

Am I doing the best I can with the precious gift of time? Could I have imagined how much my life and I would change?

April 21—When Jan and I arrive at noon, Mother, Dad, and Joy are upset. Dana, the home-care aide, is gone, threatening not to return.

It turns out that Mother had requested that Dana open and read a piece of priority mail from one of her granddaughters. Dad made a terrible scene, insisting that Dana had no right to do that. She should have waited for his return so he could read it to Mother. Jan and I tell him that it is Mother's choice. The letter is addressed to her.

Dad obviously feels outnumbered. He is used to being in charge, and Mother's reactions are out of his control. I think everything will continue to be a crisis because he feels so helpless. He latches onto every possible issue in an effort to regain some semblance of power.

Mother insists that Jan and I divide her jewelry today. Later in the afternoon, Jan's daughter and my daughter and granddaughter arrive, and we finish the task together, choosing pieces for each woman in the family.

Dad seems to be okay with her giving away her property this time. Since the fiasco over the sewing objects, he has remembered that when his father was killed in a car accident, they buried him wearing a certain tie clasp. Dad still values the matching cuff links. Joy reminds him that the bond he feels when he wears those cuff links is what Mother wants to establish with her daughters and granddaughters.

Does the fear of being forgotten spring from our minds— or from the depth of our being?

It feels eerie, dividing up belongings of someone still living, but Mother seems very happy. Perhaps she is making statements that she doesn't know how to make verbally. She weeps, tears of joy and sadness, and asks that we remember her when we wear the jewelry.

As if we could forget. . .

On Dividing the Jewelry

*T*he afternoon sun filtered through the sheer curtains as they fluttered gently in the April breeze. The tiny faces of Mother's violets lit up the windowsill. The oxygen tank "squooshed" in its corner.

We all crowded around her bed in the dining room—her only sister, her two daughters, two of her three grand-daughters, and one of her great-granddaughters.

She had called us together to give us her jewelry. She didn't have a lot of expensive pieces, especially since Dad had declared her wedding rings and his personal gifts to her off-limits. (I'm not sure he had the right to make such a declaration, but we didn't question him.)

The entire afternoon was a strange mix of festivity and sadness—a definitive example of a bittersweet moment.

With our heads bent over the jewelry boxes, we admired each piece as we lifted it out. And as we decided who would receive it, we shared the recent events in our lives as if it were any Friday afternoon. We chattered as women have through the ages—in the marketplace, over tea, as they work together.

It didn't really matter what we said—we were gathered. We understood how important it was to draw strength from four generations of womankind. We were doing more than just choosing lovely pieces of jewelry to wear with remembrance. It was a sacred rite of passage.

Mother beamed with pleasure as we cherished her treasures—delighted to give these last gifts. She flushed with excitement as her girls giggled together.

We have drawn near to help our parents and each other in these final days. We will do what has to be done. We embrace each other in love and support.

For a little while, we forget about death.

A Tiny Tear

Sometimes a tiny tear
ventures from my scrunched-shut eyes
and quietly charts
a solitary path
down my cheek

But the unshed tears
are choking me
filling every crevice
of my body and my soul

It would be better if somehow
they could freely flow
leaving empty space
and a fresh-washed peace
inside

April 22—Les and I take Mother's sister and youngest brother to Colorado Springs to visit another brother in the nursing home there. His Parkinson's disease is no better; his neck is lumpy with tumors.

When we return, I prepare Mother for bed, cleaning her up and changing her diaper.

Dad has never relented about the diapers, but when Mother asked for something to keep her dry and comfortable, my aunt bought some and quietly began using them.

April 25—For some reason Mother can't hear, and her right hand is very swollen, although she seems to be no worse otherwise. This is not a good place to plateau.

April 27—I share several new poems with Mother. She smiles even as she weeps: "You say what I wish to say, but have no words."

Perhaps we are more connected than I have thought. Or perhaps she feels connected and I am the one who is left wandering lost in the night, not yet ready to let go.

Her small frame has shrunk to almost nothing.

April 30—Mother's hearing is almost entirely gone. How dreadful to be isolated in a world of silence, unable to hear words of comfort.

It is also difficult for her to see because she is so thin that her glasses won't stay on her face. In an effort to find some way to communicate, I write in big letters on large pieces of paper with magic marker. She can easily read that, and we actually have a good conversation, although I have to remind her several times, "*You* can talk and *I* can hear."

There is nothing wrong with her mind. Thank God.

I Was Not Meant to See

The diapers were not changed today
To each inquiry she had replied
"I am still dry"

And now the skin is red and raw
the hair is matted
I gag as I bend over her

I do what I was not meant to do
I see what I was not meant to see

In the far recesses of my mind
somehow I recall that dark passage

I remember being a small infant
crying for her milk and love

I remember being her child—
Now she is mine

I see what I was not meant to see
I do what I was not meant to do

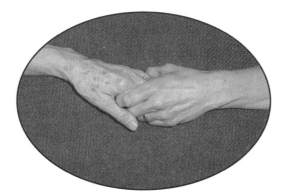

"Hands"

Photo by Connie Rempel

I'll Hold Your Hand Until You Sleep

May 4—The rain stops and the clouds lift. The world sparkles anew as I drive to see Mother. My cousin is bringing his father from the nursing home to see Mom for the last time. It is no easy task, considering my uncle's infirmities.

When I meet them at the house, I see my dying mother holding hands with her failing brother—his wheelchair close to her bed. He can barely talk and she still cannot hear, so I write notes back and forth for them on the white sheets of paper.

He insists on writing one note himself. His handwriting is so small and shaky that I can barely read it. Of course, it might be easier if my eyes were dry.

I ask him what else he wants to say to Mother. From somewhere in the twisted recesses of a brain marred by Parkinson's, where fact and fantasy now live side by side, he tells us this story:

> We were at a camp yesterday. I don't know what we were doing there. Then I noticed that they seemed to be breaking camp. Everyone was leaving, one by one. It was very sad. Everything was dwindling.

The facts were confused—the message was not. Time held up a mirror today. When I looked through the glass, I saw the future and it was I.

What If. . . ?

Sometimes I wonder if Mom heard "cancer" and simply gave up too soon.

What if she had been given antidepressant medication in February when we first found that the cancer had spread? Could that have enabled her to continue functioning for several additional months? Would the time she has been tethered to the actual dying process have been shorter?

Or was her body just too tired? Did waiting seem more tenable than fighting? When she went to bed early on, did she simply make a choice—*I will do this my way*?

What if I had been able to break through her denial—could she have shared her fears? Could I have allayed them? Would a better understanding of her particular cancer have allowed her to pursue life for another month or so? It seemed to me her only thought was that she was dying and it may well be tomorrow.

What if I had tried harder to penetrate her defenses in the year between the first diagnosis of metastatic adenocarcinoma and her current illness? Whenever I tried to talk about cancer and her feelings, she pushed me away. Perhaps I was still trying to make everything all right. Perhaps I was trying to provide the perfect dying process and death from my point of view.

Obviously, it would not have been fair to tear away her defenses. We cannot compel others to meet their death in a way we would choose. Do we have any idea what we would choose?

I have encouraged her to express her feelings, but inwardness was her choice. I wanted her to do it my way, but she counted on me to accept her where she was.

Mother once told me—as I struggled with the limitations of CFS, breast cancer, and osteoporosis—that if I wanted to be well, I would be. It was hard to hear such a judgment from her when what I needed was her support. Remembering this raised additional questions.

Did she think that by insisting that her original manifestation of cancer had been only a small problem in her knee, she could protect herself from its spread?

Did she feel that if she said she didn't have cancer, it would go away?

Was she devastated when she discovered that the premise on which she was banking her life did not hold up to the test of time?

What if. . . ? It is a timeless question and offers no more comfort to me than it has to the multitudes before me.

But I can't keep from asking it.

I'll Hold Your Hand Until You Sleep

I'll hold your hand until you sleep
you who have often held mine

I'll sit by your bed
until your last breath is drawn
holding my breath each time
as I wait for you
to breathe once more
frantically wishing for it to be over
fervently wishing to keep you forever

I'll hold your hand
until you sleep
and soothe your brow

      until it turns to stone. . .
      until it turns to stone. . .

May 8—I see Dad struggling to maintain his composure and graciousness. Last night, two of my cousins delivered a stereo and some tapes Mother had specifically requested. For whatever reason, Dad considered such a gift to be inappropriate.

Instead of accepting it in the spirit it was given and quietly setting it aside, he exploded, "How dare you come at a time like this? Don't bring music in here. This woman is *dying*. Go. Go. Go!"

Then he had to deal with his rudeness as well as his misery at feeling his private world was being overturned.

How difficult it must be to have one's home invaded. He has been overrun by family, hordes of visitors, nurses, aides, an oxygen machine, a hospital bed, diapers, cancer— and dying.

May 9—Dad tells me that two days ago he discovered a funeral plan Mother constructed with a granddaughter several weeks ago. He says that finding that document was the first time he actually believed Mother is going to die, and the first time he realized she knows it. This may explain the outburst yesterday.

Cancer and dying bring a real loss of control. Could any of us keep our composure and graciousness in the midst of all that? For people who treasure their privacy, invasion is yet another loss added to the legion.

May 10—I can visit with Mother a bit today because she has a headset to help her hear better, but she is too short of breath to talk much. I play the organ and Dad sings for her. It is a special time. I cry as I walk home.

May 12—I almost decided not to meet Joy at the house. I am getting ready for the big Spring Recital on Sunday as well as our trip to Oklahoma City on Friday and I'm rattled with all the details. At the last minute, I go anyway.

Joy's face is serious as she checks Mother. She beckons Dad and me into the kitchen. "There are significant changes," she says. "It may not be today, but it will surely be very soon."

Dad and I just sit there. My eyes fill with tears. His shoulders droop.

Joy explains that our only job now is to keep her comfortable. The care will be very simple. Joy leaves a bottle of morphine to relieve Mother's feeling of suffocation. We are to put several drops under Mother's tongue whenever we notice that her struggle to breathe draws in the skin at her collarbone. Joy leaves a prescription for a refill.

I have known for months that Mom is dying, but it is as if I hear the news for the first time. Even though I want to stay by her side every moment now, I go to the church to practice for the recital Sunday. Karen stays; she wants to have some private time with her grandmother.

I decide to play "How Great Thou Art" at the recital as a tribute to Mother. My God! Have I made the transition from attempting to stave off her death to honoring her with hymns?

Last Words

I didn't mean to cry—
I promised not to cry—

But as I held her hand and
watched her try so hard to breathe,
suddenly I lay my head
on her soft breast
and sobbed.

The warmth of her body
and the sweet fragrance of her skin
enveloped me.

She strained to pull
her emaciated arms
from under the covers
to form a gentle circle
around me.

I felt the faintest flutter
of her bird-like hands
and I knew
she was patting me.

It's okay to cry, she said.
It will be all right, she said.

And there in that
circle of love, it was.

For one brief, luminous moment
It truly was all right. . .

May 14—I am grateful I have the presence of mind to get up early and pack everything I'll need for the big Spring Piano Recital and Graduation Recital this afternoon. I am thankful that I decide at the last minute to go help Jan bathe Mother before Les and I go to the church.

We set everything up; the first program goes beautifully. During the reception between the two concerts, Renée comes to tell us that Mother's condition is deteriorating rapidly. Her respirations are only three per minute. Although I desert the five precious girls who are giving their last recital, my only thought is to get to Mom in time.

Joy had told us Friday that we were to keep her comfortable, giving her morphine as often as we noticed retraction. It would, as promised, relieve her sensation of suffocation and the struggling respiration. It is very efficient to give it in tiny amounts at short intervals. Karen prepares the medication; Nick watches for retraction; I administer the doses. The rest of the family keeps watch.

It is hard to continue giving morphine, knowing that it might hasten her death, but we have pledged that she will not suffer. Sometimes her teeth are clenched shut and I agonize that I am forcing her.

From 4:00 in the afternoon until 11:58, my eyes never leave her face and I am taking her pulse as it gradually fades, then stops. Her eyes are open, but she isn't looking at us—her gaze focuses beyond us, and it is clear that she sees that which we cannot.

And so, on this Mother's Day, my beloved mother dies.

I gently close her mouth and hold her chin in place until it stays. I tuck the covers around her. She looks more peaceful than she has for eleven weeks—maybe more peaceful than she ever has.

We wait in silent good-bye, hearts breaking, until 2:35 a.m. when two men from the crematory come to take her body. They wrap her in a white sheet, twist the ends shut, and carry her out.

Dear God, I have no mother.

Eulogy

And so she dies as she has lived—
safely in her home
surrounded by

cookbooks,
African violets, her paintings,
and her family

Did I Miss Something?

As she lowered herself
onto the edge of the hospice bed
that last time and slowly
swung her legs around,
did she understand
that she was claiming
her deathbed?

Surely she could not have guessed
the indignities that awaited her there

Surely she could not have fathomed
how her body would betray her there

Surely she could not have known
that in the wee hours one morning
two respectful men
in ill-fitting black suits
would spin her into a cocoon of white sheet
and carry her out into the dark

Surely she could not have dreamed
how long it would take—
that snowfall would turn to rain
that Lent would come and go
that crocus would give way to primrose

It was simply a matter of lying there
between the delicate peach sheets
in her pale lavender gown
her white hair fanned across the pillow—
with no mobility, no autonomy, no hope

It was simply a matter of
slowly, slowly saying good-bye
      to everyone
      to everything
      to everywhere

Yet sometimes she smiled
yet somehow she smiled

Maybe she knew something
I don't know. . .

The author and her mother

Motherless Child

Firstborn

Until my birth
she had been
a childless mother

Upon her death
I have become
a motherless child

May 18—I can't believe the things I'm writing. The memorial service is today. I can't even believe she has died. I'm not sure what one is supposed to do on the day of a funeral, but I frantically try to finish up my deskwork, pack for a speaking tour, and make final preparations for the service.

I wish I could just sit in the rocking chair with my arms wrapped around myself, rocking, holding myself together.

The service is beautiful—the songs and scriptures she had planned, the homily, the tributes from her children. Dad's sweet tenor voice quavers only slightly as he sings "Be Still, My Soul."

I wonder if she's pleased?

Small Miracle

Pictures of Mother and her family
cluster on the "memory" table.

Her handiwork is
both background and drape—
the quilt she pieced,
the cream afghan from the sofa,
a fluffy pink baby blanket
that has been waiting
in the cedar chest. . .

Just yesterday
we had news—
our anticipated grandchild
will be a little girl. . .

A Timely Death

It was not an
untimely death—
as dying goes
it was about as timely as
one can get.

She lived a long life.

She languished in bed
only eleven weeks—
managing to die
just soon enough for me
to attend her service
Thursday evening and still
leave for Oklahoma City
Friday morning.

Dad even got to go
to Lions Club
Tuesday noon.

We could sit at her bedside
and share in her death
because it was Sunday
and no one had anywhere else to be.

No, it was not
an untimely death.
It fit the schedule well—

Only my heart was taken
completely by surprise.

I Clutch the Keys

My mother held the keys
to what I can't remember

She was the buffer
between eternity and me

She was the one
who first gave love

Now—against my will—
I am at the head of the line

I lead the way to
the new tomorrow

I clutch the keys
to the memories
my children
can't remember

I give the love
that can't be bought

At last I am first—
I'd rather be second again.

July 21—As usual, I have Friday lunch with Dad at the house. Everything is the same—the sandwiches, the chocolates and peanuts, the places we sit. Mother is not there.

July 28—Les and I take Dad out for lunch. He is having an especially hard day. He can't believe Mother would leave him alone to do everything. He isn't thinking of remarrying, but he really needs a companion. He thinks one of my friends should be it. She is even younger than I. This is *really* a cry of pain.

September 4—We eat on the patio this evening. Dad is with us. He seems more lonely and sad. He comments, "You can only do so much running."

Childhood Home

When I lost my mother
somehow I lost
my childhood home

Father always greets me
at the door—
        hat in hand
        eager to escape
        ready to run

I feel quite sure that if
I could only get inside
I would find her—
        by the African violets
        near her teacup collection
        in the closet still filled
        with clothes and gentle scent

Maybe he knows something
I don't know. . .

"Mother's Chair"

Photo by Connie Rempel

Please Call
Security

When I Leave

When I travel
sometimes I lose the thread
I don't always remember
that she is dead

As the miles zip by
I imagine her at home
waiting for me

I can pretend
that I have left—
not she. . .

September 20—Today is Mother's birthday. It is a busy day for me. I have a presentation at 9:00 a.m. at Southwest Medical Center here in Oklahoma City, a luncheon speech at Baptist Medical Center, and a reading at 5:30 p.m. before the Board of Directors of the Oklahoma City Chapter of the Komen Foundation. I am especially pleased about the Komen Foundation meeting since they do so much to help breast cancer patients—in education, research, and support.

I wonder briefly if my overscheduling the day has anything to do with the birthday.

After Les and I fight the rain one last time and return to the hotel, weary and cold, I feel let down. I've been hoping against hope that our new grandchild, due next week, would arrive on Mom's birthday.

I try to call Keith and Kara several times, but the line is busy. It is already 10:30 p.m. I check my messages and there isn't even one saying that they have gone to the hospital. Kara's first labor was very long. I know it is too late. It is simply too late.

Fifteen minutes later, the phone rings. Keith says, "We did it. We have our little girl."

On Mother's birthday? Was Kirsten Nicole really born on Mother's birthday? Oh, joy of joy!

The circle of life continues.

Will Someone Please Call Security?

We are rushing to meet
the checkout deadline
when I grab the jewelry bag
from my purse and
carelessly toss it
into the suitcase.

It is the little fabric bag
Mother bought at a bazaar
and gave to me last Christmas—
a very practical gift.

I toss it into the suitcase—
and here in Houston, Texas,
in the Doubletree Hotel
at 11:36 in the morning
my grief overtakes me.

The little drawstring bag
snuggles into a corner
of the suitcase.

The sudden reality
of my mother's death
tears out a corner
of my heart. . .

September 28—As Les and I return from yet another trip to Oklahoma and Texas, we stop at the cemetery in Joes, Colorado, where my grandparents and great-grandparents are buried. Somehow, seeing their graves brings new poignancy to my grief. When we go out to the old farmstead, I realize anew that Mother did hold the keys to memories I don't have.

October 1—It is my first birthday without my mother. Les and I visit Dad awhile. It is one of the few times I have been in the house since Mom's funeral. It startles me to see her apron still hanging on the railing of the back stairs.

But Can I Hide?

Anxious to get the grieving done
I run and run and run and run

Thinking at last I'm almost there
I glimpse her apron hanging,
still hanging, hanging
by the stair

November 1—My uncle's funeral is simple but lovely. Well, maybe *lovely* isn't quite the word. I knew all of Mother's family when they were young and I find it incredibly hard to see them going one by one.

It is miserably cold at the cemetery. Then Dad wants to go to the mausoleum where Mother's ashes lie to "see her and tell her that her brother is there with her." She probably knows.

November 23—I weep when I accidentally set the Thanksgiving table for two too many; I weep when I put out the place cards and run across "Mother" and "Uncle Paul." I weep when Dad arrives alone; I weep as we hold hands and say grace.

December 25—The Christmas candle we lit this morning burned out about 10:00 p.m. This first Christmas without Mom is finally over. I raise my fist and whisper, "Yes!"

December 31—The year is history. It seems strange to greet a new year that Mother will never know.

February 22—We just pulled into the driveway moments ago. Les struggles with our suitcases, the snack case, the map bag, a basket of half-dead tulips, and two new Teddy bears. I open the blinds and turn up the thermostat.

We have returned from another sixteen nights of waking in various strange beds, wondering in the dim light where the bathroom is. The endless miles of dreary February landscape (except for the herd of camels north of Fort Worth) offered endless opportunities to contemplate, to ruminate, and to assimilate new experiences, as well as old.

As we traveled, I wondered again how Mother would have handled our constant travel if she were still alive. Many times she had expressed the thought that I had done enough. How would she have felt about these long absences?

I know how I feel. I savor the highlights and the lowlights that become highlights. I am grateful for the certainty that each visit is to the right place and at the right time.

It was a typical trip in a long string of trips. It was a good trip. I put the bedraggled tulips on the kitchen table and start supper.

February 23—It is a year ago today that Mother was admitted to the hospital for radiation therapy after a bone scan confirmed that her lung cancer was active. I take Dad to lunch. When I drop him off, I run into the house to use the bathroom.

I glance at the window where her violets still bloom profusely. (Dad has faithfully cared for them, replacing each one when it dies.) Her apron has not been moved. Suddenly, her absence overwhelms me again.

I hide my tears until I get back into the car, away from Dad's sad eyes.

As I drive away, I recognize that lately I have been remembering the things I didn't like about her. Of course, we had issues—most mothers and daughters do—but I have been dwelling on her deficiencies. I have thought more often of the times she seemed manipulative or uncaring.

What do they call this phase—the end of idealization, the return to reality? We set up expectations of others that we don't share with them or even acknowledge to ourselves. Then we are disappointed when they don't meet them.

Somehow I have convinced myself that perhaps I don't miss her as much as I have thought. Is it a way to circumvent the pain?

Now I contemplate some of the things I desperately miss—Mother's delight in seeing me, the comforting talks, the sunshine in her living room as we sat in a companionable silence, the new recipes, the confidences we shared. And I ponder the things *she* has missed in this year—the new babies [four great-grandchildren], the family events, a year of life.

I think about how her clothes still hang in the closet. I think about how life has just gone on without her. And I acknowledge what I have lost.

God, I miss my mother.

The Secret

The jagged edges of grief
tear at my spirit
they pull and snag
and rip and shred

Is there a secret to
surviving with
the fabric of my life
somewhat intact?

"The Homestead"

Painted by the author's mother

Where Can I Find Her?

August 9—Jan and I meet at Dad's house. For well over a year now, he has sporadically announced that he would be ready to deal with Mom's clothing right after the next landmark had passed. First, it was after their anniversary; next, it was as soon as the yard work was over; then, "Let's get the holidays behind us"; finally, it was the anniversary of her death. Between times, I would occasionally ask if he were ready yet. Neither Jan nor I found ourselves pushing much—we were no more anxious to tackle the task than he.

People would say, "He hasn't discarded her things *yet*?" But we didn't care if he let them hang there forever. We knew eventually the job would fall to us and we were willing to wait.

As we venture into the closets, it is uncanny to think about those clothes hanging there for fifteen months. Some of them are soiled, but, of course, she hadn't known she wouldn't be wearing them again. She would have been embarrassed to leave clothes dirty in a closet for so long.

We hold back several pieces, either for ourselves or our daughters, but most of her garments are old and out of style.

After some initial tears, our anal German heritage takes the upper hand and we make short work of the packing.

Where Can I Find Her?

Where can I find my mother?
Will she somehow live on in me?

Will I wear her pewter cross
as a talisman?

Will I find sympathy
in the tea from
her bone china cups?

Will I glimpse my soul
in the landscape
of her paintings?

Will the many afghans
finally warm my heart?

Will I someday learn
to mother myself?

Can I wrap my arms
around that small child
who was born old,
who never had a childhood,
who was me?

August 20—I speak in a small Texas community to a group of breast cancer survivors. The commonness of our plight, our journey, our mission enables us to form an instant bond. We don't need days or weeks or months to build a relationship. Perhaps our shared experience brings us a heightened sense of sisterhood that transcends the moment.

I don't know the answer. I only know that it causes me pain each time I reluctantly walk away from these encounters. I feel a physical tearing of the tenuous ties that bind us and while my spirit is enriched to link with other survivors, my heart is diminished to leave.

I've thought of ways to reach hundreds of children and thousands of women. Why couldn't I reach my own mother?

How could I have lived with my mother all of my life and never felt as close to her as I do to these women I have barely met?

Or is my perception wrong—regarding them, regarding my mother?

September 17—It is the final morning of a twenty-four-day speaking trip to New England and the East Coast. Although rain pelted the car for 670 miles yesterday, the sky is clear. The road is smooth.

We are traversing the western half of Kansas and the eastern half of Colorado.

Again we pass through Joes, Colorado, my mother's birthplace. I remember the pleasant summers we spent with her parents—the sandbox (always filled with fresh sand from the creek) under the mulberry trees, long summer evenings on the old oak bench swing in the screened porch, fresh country eggs for breakfast, mothering my young siblings and cousins, picnics in the Sand Hills. My mother's presence still pervades this bleak and beautiful land. The land and she seep into my heart.

The thousands and thousands of miles have been arduous. The constancy of the traffic, the intricacies of the many interstate highways, the press of the foliage in the East, the overwhelming presence of trucks and speeding red cars, the many speaking engagements have daunted me.

All I want to do is ride in silence and memory, soaking up the vastness of sky and horizon—the absence, the infinity.

It is the very economy of scenery, of color, of stimulation that soothes my spirit. After so many days of "way too much," it is "way too little" that restores my soul.

November 15—I stand in the grocery store, sorting through some grapes that have seen better days. Tears stream down my face. *She's never coming back. She's really never coming back.*

With a start, I acknowledge that I have not finished grieving. I'm not sure I have even identified all the losses. My life has been too harried in these months since she is gone. There have been distractions.

People say, "One does what one has to do."

People say, "One deals with the hand one is dealt."

And yet, the grief seems so fresh—her loss so permanent.

On Missed Connections

*F*or the last several years of her life, I devoted my Fridays to Les' mother, Mary. I brought groceries for her, did her hair, and shared lunch with her. When my mother complained, I promised that her time was next.

After Mary died, Mother and I had four years of Friday lunches before Dad's retirement. We shared more during that time than we had—or ever would again. She often said, "I look forward to our Fridays."

After Dad retired, we continued our Friday lunches. However, with Dad joining us at the kitchen table, our conversations became more general. The sweet rhythm of those quiet afternoons never quite returned.

For twenty-five years, Friday was our day. I shopped with her and for her. I helped her with fall cleaning. Together we crocheted intricate afghans for our grandchildren. The time spent was not a sacrifice; I treasured those visits with her.

Yet no matter how much time I spent, she wanted more. Sometimes I felt she was ungrateful when she begged me to stay. I have always been busy—raising four children, teaching music, coping with breast cancer, writing *Fine Black Lines*, and now speaking to cancer survivors.

Sometimes I felt an afternoon was wasted, especially if we just made small talk or she was particularly cross with Dad or me. Sometimes I simply needed to be other places, doing other things.

While Mother lived, I missed her and yearned for a stronger connection. I longed to tear down the barriers between us and partake of the pain and joy that truth and compassion can bring. Since her death, I miss her even more. Sometimes the lost opportunities overwhelm me.

I used to want to shake her into being real with me; now I want to pull her back from the ashes and insist that we tell one another the truth.

What prevented us from attaining a deeper bond?

Did her heritage make her reticent to discuss personal things and be open with feelings? Was it because I never felt I could be totally honest with her?

In many subtle ways she pressed for reassurance. She would ask if she'd been a good mother. I always said, "Yes," being the good daughter, protecting both of us from the truth, missing the opportunity to develop an honest relationship.

Then she'd say wistfully, "All these people who have to visit psychiatrists because of their parents. . . I couldn't bear it if that happened to one of my children." She assumed it would mean she had failed. I never did tell her about the years I spent in therapy—searching my soul.

How Could I Tell Her?

How could I tell
my beloved mother
who needed love and affirmation
even more than another

that her quest for perfection tainted me
that her disdain for my father burdened me
that her necessity to sermonize silenced me?

How could I tell her the truth?

On Missed Connections
(concluded)

I take some comfort in having made a valiant effort to get past those perceived barriers, yet I was never fully honest with her. I didn't want to hurt her and I didn't want to hear her say, "It's your own fault."

The fact remains that the links were not there. I felt I began to understand her better when I became a mother myself and again when I began to face various issues of aging, but some of the ties broke down through her refusal to battle cancer together.

I cannot rearrange the past realities to meet my needs. I cannot reinvent who she was so that I can reorder my memories and extricate my pain. I cannot go back and forge those missing links.

Can I simply treasure her gifts? Can I embrace what she has left me, gently cup my hands, and pour what was best about her into the outstretched hands of those who follow?

Can I just let her go?

Can I forgive us both?

Perplexity

Do I weep for her—
for me—

for the relationship
that might have been

and now will never be?

"Benediction"

Painted by the author's mother

Beyond Regret

May 11—It is Mother's Day again. I can't believe it has been two years since Mom died. Neither can I believe I'll be speaking in Garden City, New York, tomorrow evening.

The drive through New York City is beautiful—flowering trees and shrubs everywhere. I am thinking about Mom a lot—and about cancer.

After I was diagnosed with breast cancer, Mother seemed to shrink back from me as if to ward off a blow that she feared would be mortal. In a way, I began to lose her then. . .

Did I represent a threat to her trust that God would keep her children safe? She prayed for us daily. How could this have happened to a daughter who was to be her protector, who was to be her safety net for the future?

Did I threaten her faith in positive thinking? She was angry when I didn't or couldn't express positive thoughts. She was upset when I tried to express reality as I perceived it. She upbraided me for not trying harder to be well. She began to divorce herself from me emotionally and to turn to my healthier sister.

When Mother was diagnosed with lung cancer, the reality of my disease seemed to frighten her even more. Did I represent mortality, suffering, loss—all that she wanted to deny?

She seemed to feel I betrayed her by becoming ill, and although she may have wished to forgive me, I'm not sure she ever could. Have I forgiven her for preempting my disease and turning it into the vehicle of her final abandonment?

Yes, I lost my mother to cancer—hers, and mine. On this Mother's Day, I long for her.

I Never Much Liked Mother's Day

I never much liked Mother's Day—
expectations high,
reality never quite measuring up.

One year I brought a red rose,
but it wasn't right—
her mother was already dead
so it was supposed to be white.

Another year Mother only wanted
"all my children and grandchildren
sitting around me in church."

I barely delivered—
my thirteen-year-old
protested every step of the way,
all the rest of the day,
on into a new century.

Several times I wondered
where I fit into the picture—
I bore four children myself.

Was homage something she required
or something I felt compelled to provide?

I'll never know,
but on the day she died
Mother's Day was ruined forever—
I can no longer bear to touch a rose. . .

On Questions Unasked

When I first knew Mother was terminally ill, someone told me that I should ask her everything I wanted to know.

For the most part, I lost that opportunity. In those stressful weeks, I could not find the questions. She did not have the strength to respond with the answers. I felt upset when I recognized that I was not availing myself of the ever-shortening time, but it is only now that I begin to realize with what finality that door to my history is closed.

Part of my medical history is lost. From what illnesses did my ancestors die? I don't know if there was breast cancer in my family history. People didn't talk about such things. I have an early memory of getting some sort of x-ray treatment. For what? How much?

Why didn't I ask these questions?

Could, or would, she have answered?

The door to my emotional history is closed, too. The anecdotes I'm not able to remember are permanently forgotten. The various quirks of my grandparents that only she might have explained are locked out. Half-memories that only she could help refresh, become dimmer.

I don't even know why she named me Lois Luene.

November 28—The third Christmas without Mother is fast approaching. My ten-year-old granddaughter comes to help me put up the Christmas decorations. It is one of our grandmother-granddaughter traditions.

The tree in the living room is natural; we use pinecones, wooden decorations, and clear lights. The bedroom tree with its red and gold miniature packages is all ready when we pull off the tree blanket. I don't undecorate it each year.

But the tree in the piano studio downstairs is another matter. Its adornments are strictly sentimental; we decorate it with memories, not color schemes or categories. As we pull out each special ornament, I tell Emily where I got it and why it is important. Actually, she's heard the stories so many times that she repeats them to *me*.

Many of the ornaments are gifts from piano students over the years. There is another box of carefully wrapped, beautiful glass ornaments that once trimmed the tree in my childhood home.

Mother made many of the other items—the delicate hand-crocheted snowflakes; the various shapes intricately embellished with tiny beads; the counted-thread fabric ornaments. They are astonishing expressions of her artistic abilities and her patience with complicated craft projects.

Finally, the lovely memory tree glistens—each object arranged almost as tastefully as Emily's great-grandmother might have done it. Emily and I sigh with pride, switch on the lights, and step back to admire our handiwork.

December 27—Dad brings Mother's diary to me. He just found it on the stand beside her chair in a black leather zipper bag. It has been there all along, but he hadn't realized what it was until he looked inside. I am thrilled.

I pour a cup of tea, sit in my favorite chair by the big window, and read. The diary consists mainly of very brief entries—a weather report, guests visiting, birth dates of grandchildren, data on numerous weddings, notations of ever more numerous deaths.

Comments are sparse—unrevealing. Once she mentioned that one of my recitals was "great!" When a granddaughter told her about an impending divorce, she wrote, "Bad news!" After recording a luncheon date with a friend, she observed, "Very enjoyable." The most emotional entry says, "Jan's car accident. Thank God she wasn't hurt!"

The day I told Mother and Dad about my upcoming surgery, she simply wrote: "Lois informs us that she has breast cancer." My second mastectomy fourteen months later is never mentioned.

The final page, begun at the first intimation of her own cancer, reads as follows:

> ***December 26***—*Severe pain in left leg below knee.*
>
> ***December 27***—*To Dr. D___. Suggested I see Dr. W___, a tumor specialist, who did biopsy—found malignancy. Spent the night in the hospital.*
>
> ***December 28***—*Came home from hospital. Feeling much better.*
>
> ***January 1 to 7***—*Spent week having tests and x-rays. Found my body clean!*
>
> ***January 12***—*Appointment with Dr. G____, oncologist. Gave me options. We decided on radiation.*
>
> ***January 20***—*Appointment with Dr. H_____. First radiation treatment of series of fifteen.*
>
> ***January 24***—*Huberts [long-time friends] came for birthday celebrations. Went to Furr's Cafeteria for dinner.*
>
> ***January 25***—*Huberts left to return to Loveland. I had fourth treatment.*

Tears trickle down my cheeks. I contemplate what might have been on those pages had she continued to write during her final fifteen months. What would she have written on those empty lines, or added to the lines that were not empty, had she chosen to articulate her feelings, had she been able to find the words?

I Wrap Myself in Love

I wrap myself in Mother's quilted housecoat. I remember how uncharacteristically pleased she was that she had been able to sew a beautiful housecoat at age eighty-four. Somehow, in its warmth and security, I feel her arms about me.

I have thought long and hard about our relationship—about my responsibility to keep us connected. My ambivalence follows me into my grief.

Part of the regret I feel has to do with the marriage of my parents. An overarching reality of my life has been that my parents were there for me in their own way, yet their disconnection from each other somehow disconnected me from them.

It was many, many years before I realized that what I knew of their marriage was mainly what they had chosen to reveal.

As the oldest child, I struggled to make everything okay. I have figured out at long last that I really didn't need to do that, that I couldn't do that. I am sorry that Mother was sometimes unable to give Dad the warmth and support he craved, that my father all too rarely saw and treated Mother as an equal partner. I am sorry, but it was their relationship. They did the best they could.

The larger regret I feel has to do with Mother herself. I was well aware that she was disappointed that I did not meet all of her expectations.

All my life, I was very uncomfortable when I hurt her feelings. As a teenager, angry words of conflict rang in my ears many mornings as I walked to school. I always called from a pay phone to apologize. I couldn't stand to think about her crying, especially if I felt I was the reason.

It was only after I had teenagers—and then teenaged grandchildren—that I recognized the separation process often involves conflict. I certainly had not understood it before. My mother never seemed to understand that.

As a young wife and mother, I felt flawed because I knew that no matter how much I tried, I could not meet Mother's standards of perfection—children who spoke only when spoken to, white-glove cleanliness, a stoicism that left private feelings undisclosed. I lived in a different time.

I often felt she needed me to validate her life and her choices. But from the time I was a young girl, deciding on where I wanted to sit on a Good Friday afternoon, I felt a powerful need to forge my own life and make my own choices.

In later years, I imagined that perhaps, if I visited her every week, I could fill the void I sensed in her life.

And during her final illness, I hoped that if I were at her bedside every day, if I complied with her every request, if I thought of every possibility to make her feel comfortable and safe—no matter whether or not I got a sign of approval from her—I would know that I had done everything I could. In this final instance, perhaps I could at least meet my own expectations. But that was another of life's fantasies.

I wish our companionship could have been deeper. I would like to have shared more of my spiritual journey, without worrying that she was judging me. I wish I could have faced some of our issues without her feeling threatened. I would like to have helped her view life as an imperfect journey to enjoy rather than as a perfect destination for which to strive.

I would dearly love to have provided more comfort in her life, even as I longed for her to comfort me.

It is clear I will always have regrets. Perhaps I honor her in those regrets. Had I cared less for her, I might indeed have eluded remorse.

I am older now—and wiser. I well understand that I have had the advantage of examining my life in ways her background and personality did not allow.

When my sister left home, Mother seemed to feel her life was over. She had played out her goals of motherhood and homemaking. She went through some difficult adjustments and much anxiety.

By the time Mother was in her early sixties, her anxiety medication caused her to lose touch with reality for awhile. She spent several weeks in a psychiatric hospital—wandering in a fog that her doctors and the rest of us worried might be permanent. But as the medication cleared from her system, she improved. At her doctor's behest, she went into therapy for a month or two. Then she discontinued, saying, "I think Dad is the problem. There is no reason for me to keep going if he won't go."

I tried to encourage her to continue. She was the one who was hurting. Surely understanding herself and her life a bit better would be a benefit. She didn't go back.

I cannot change how things were, but I can find solace in the truth that just because she didn't love me as I might have wanted to be loved, doesn't mean that she didn't love me with as much love as she had to give.

And I have come to a place where I can look at her flaws without feeling disloyal. I can choose the traits I wish to emulate. I can work on those I'd rather avoid. She wasn't the perfect mother she longed to be. I certainly wasn't the perfect daughter she wanted.

I do not need to pretend I am someone I am not. I do not need to pretend she was someone she wasn't. With that freedom, my dearest memories of her resurface. I can rejoice in her life. I can forgive her and hope she has somehow forgiven me.

As I gather her quilted housecoat closer to my body, Mother's love envelops me. Everything *is* all right.

It is time to move beyond disappointment, beyond all-encompassing sorrow, beyond regret—into forgiveness.

It is time to bid my mother good-bye.

I wish her Godspeed.

I Never Prayed for My Mother

In all the years I enjoyed her company,
chafed at her criticism,
thought I would have her forever,
I never prayed for my mother

Although I fervently wished
her life to be richer,
her comfort to be higher,
her courage to uphold her,
I never prayed for my mother

I pray for her now—
that she has found Paradise,
that she dances with the far-flung stars,
that, when she rests,
it is in Peace

"Dawn"

Photo by Lois Tschetter Hjelmstad

Epilogue

The mourning for Mother continued, of course, although a sense of peace overlay the landscape of grief.

Life settled into a new routine for me as a daughter. I continued to spend Friday afternoons with my father. It was a rich experience to know him as a person rather than as half of "my parents." The time was definitely not wasted; the conversations were deep and lively. Seeing Dad as an individual rather than as a father allowed us to be friends.

I only knew my mother in the context of their marriage. Had Dad died first, would my relationship with Mom have been as transformed as my relationship with Dad?

I cherished the freedom to be with Dad. When I asked him to go somewhere or have dinner, he enthusiastically agreed. My more reclusive mother had kept a note by the phone reminding her to say, when someone called with an invitation, "I'm sorry, but we have other plans."

I no longer had to choose sides in an argument. I no longer swam against the undercurrents of a marriage that I sometimes perceived as toxic, no matter what the truth might have been. I no longer worried that I was playing favorites.

During those three years, Dad and I became very close. We grieved the loss of Mother, knowing our losses were different. Our methods of coping were also different. For many months after Mother's death, Dad visited the crypt and found a great deal of comfort. Eventually, he decided she wasn't really there. I felt that the first time I went.

He supported me in my writing and speaking in a way Mother couldn't have understood. Although he clung to me each time I left on a tour, he knew why I went and he sent me off with "Good luck."

Our relationship wasn't entirely smooth, however. We struggled over estate issues and his continuing to drive. We accused each other of being stubborn. But overall, Dad and I had three priceless years that I wouldn't trade for anything.

Dad died of an aortic aneurysm, a little over three years after Mother's death. I had talked with him on the phone an hour earlier. When I went over to see why he hadn't called back as he promised, his body was already cold. He had chaired two meetings the day before and then cut his lawn in a beautiful crisscross pattern.

His ashes lie beside Mother's in the crypt he had insisted on for her.

My brother, my sister, and I have reestablished our family of origin in one another.

Distilling the traits and traditions of our past, we have secured our future.

Insight

One death with its grieving
does not ready us
for another. . .

A Birthday Mourning

A birthday morning—
an ocean shore, far from home
whitecaps blend
into the mist above
driftwood lies gray upon the sand
relics of places distant, days of yore

A birthday morning—
my first as an orphan, the woman who bore
me gone three years and more
the man who sired me, ashes encrypted

A birthday *mourning*—
for the two who gave me life

and where am I
under this threatening sky?

Who am I
and when
shall *I* die?

The Last Violet

After the estate sale,
when everyone was gone,
I stood in the middle of the living room,
more bereft than I had ever
imagined I could be.

I looked around
and there it was—the last violet—
somehow left behind,
forlornly sitting on the wide sill,
the last of Mother's garden.

I took it home,
watered it,
fed it,
talked to it,
loved it. . .

It died.

When I finally found
the courage to throw it out,
I carefully wrapped it
in white tissue paper
and apologized:

"I just can't keep you alive anymore."

Picture of parents' home

Photo by author's father

The Last Visit

I remember my last visit to my parents' house. Les waited in the car and told me to take as long as necessary. He wanted to give me the space I needed.

There were still a few pencils, a lamp, and a card table to pick up. Some autumn leaves had been tracked onto the stairs. I carefully swept them up with my hands.

I stood there in the empty rooms. The only other time I had seen the house vacant was the day we moved in, years ago.

Once again, the reel in my mind spun through the memories. I tried to grasp that it was my last visit. I barely noticed the tears on my cheeks.

Finally, I glanced up at the kitchen clock to check how late it was. The clock, of course, wasn't there.

Nothing was there. No one.

Slowly I pulled the door shut. Slowly I put my key in the lock and turned it. As I walked down the front steps for the last time, I suddenly realized it was only a *house*.

Les and I have a *home*. I slid into the car next to him—and we went there.

Appendix

The Needs of the Dying

- The need to be treated as a living human being.
- The need to maintain a sense of hopefulness, however changing its focus may be.
- The need to be cared for by those who can maintain a sense of hopefulness, however changing this may be.
- The need to express feelings and emotions about death in one's own way.
- The need to participate in decisions concerning one's care.
- The need to be cared for by compassionate, sensitive, knowledgeable people.
- The need to expect continuing medical care, even though the goals may change from "cure" to "comfort" goals.
- The need to have all questions answered honestly and fully.
- The need to seek spirituality.
- The need to be free of physical pain.
- The need to express feelings and emotions about pain in one's own way.
- The need of children to participate in death.
- The need to understand the process of death.
- The need to die in peace and dignity.
- The need not to die alone.
- The need to know that the sanctity of the body will be respected after death.

Reprinted with permission from
 "The Needs of the Dying" by David Kessler
 HarperCollins Publishers
 www.DavidKessler.org

On Choosing Hospice

When I saw Mother's hospital bed set up in the dining room, I could barely hide my dismay.

Yet, ironically perhaps, I had been interested in the hospice movement since it first came to the United States in the early 1970s. Fortunately, it has grown throughout the country so that services were accessible to us when we needed them. In 1974, there was only one hospice program in this country. By 1995, there were 2,100. In 2002, there are over 3,300 programs in the United States, the District of Columbia, the Commonwealth of Puerto Rico, and the Territory of Guam.

Stanley Marks, M. D., medical director of the Allegheny General Hospice in Pittsburgh, says:

> *Hospice attempts to maximize the quality of the patient's life when a cure is no longer possible. Our chief objectives are to control symptoms—mainly pain, nausea, and depression—to help assure patients that they will have a dignified death.*

Time and time again, hospice workers have told me that often they are not called until the very end. It is true that in order to enter hospice, a doctor must certify that a patient is presumably terminal within six months. It is also true that medical treatments for which the intent is cure are discontinued, but aggressive palliative efforts then become the focus of the medical treatment. Of course, should the unexpected happen and the patient recover, she can always check out of hospice. There is no logical reason to delay the help hospice can bring.

Isn't it better when the hospice workers have time to build supportive relationships with the patient and the family that can carry into the grieving process? Isn't it better to have the expertise of those who are familiar with the dying process readily available earlier on? Our family certainly benefited by learning how to use the tools at our disposal. We often were able to avoid or limit distressing symptoms.

When pain control is adequate and patients have been set free from the symptoms, they can deal with spiritual and emotional issues in their lives and resolve some of them. When dying patients are relieved from the discomfort that distracts them, they can come to terms with their losses and their grief. They can treasure time with the family. Often relationships become exquisite. Family members who are given the privilege of grieving together are less wounded and more able to finish grieving when the patient dies.

We learned that we could participate in the home-care program as long as home was a safe place for Mother and a capable caregiver was at hand. Although I went over to help each day, I was painfully aware that a day is twenty-four hours long. The constant care required to keep a patient at home can be overwhelming—bathing, feeding, turning, drinks of water, and numerous calls in the night. It was a miracle that my elderly father could, and would, shoulder such responsibilities.

Hospice helped with that burden. Most hospice patients/families have trained volunteers assigned who often supply tremendous respite support for the family and can play an integral role in assisting the patient in the psychosocial aspects of the journey.

For two hours each day, Mother's home-care aide, Dana, came to bathe her, change the bed linens, and do whatever else she could to make Mother comfortable and content.

Three times a week, Joy, the competent nurse assigned to Mother, checked in. She was the one who comforted us; upon whose words we hung; upon whose shoulder we leaned. Dad was sure he didn't need or want to confer with the social worker, but one was available and ready to help, as was the chaplain.

Hospice workers, unlike the rest of us, know that sometimes they have to offer information and then let the patients and family ask questions. The hard part is waiting until they are ready. Some never are.

Hospice workers strive to come into someone's home and be at ease without seeming to walk in as if it is their turf.

They wish to be available, but not invasive. Leave *that* to the cancer. They want to bring information and practical suggestions as well as physical and emotional comfort.

In our particular hospice program, we were assured that should short-term respite-care in the residential hospice unit be needed, it was available. Final in-hospice care would have been an option had it become too difficult to continue home-care.

I have asked many hospice workers across the country how they can deal with terminal situations over and over. Without fail they have replied that although it is, of course, difficult to lose each person, they receive much more than they give.

One hospice nurse told me how gratified she feels to know she has contributed something to people in the most difficult situation they've ever faced. It is her personal belief that one cannot repeatedly deal with the mortality of others unless one attempts to deal with one's own.

A nurse in Nebraska said, "It is very rewarding when I have helped patients to maintain a decent quality of life and *to die as they had hoped, not as they had feared.* My patients have taught me deep lessons about the fragility of life and the strength of love."

Hospice also provides comfort after death has occurred. For many months, I was distressed about the administration of morphine to my mother at such close intervals. It was also very unsettling to me that she clamped her mouth shut. I almost felt I was compelling her to take it. I was relieved to learn, albeit much later, that at a certain level of consciousness, a person clamps her mouth shut if it is touched, similar to what a baby does.

The hospice nurse also reassured me that shortening Mother's life by an hour or so at that point was irrelevant. We had promised to keep her comfortable.

Our family was significantly helped by hospice. Mother's wish to die at home, without pain, with dignity, was fulfilled.

Hospice and Cancer Organizations

Alliance for Lung Cancer Advocacy
Support and Education
1601 Lincoln Avenue
Vancouver, WA 98660
800.298.2436

American Cancer Society, Inc.
National Home Office
1599 Clifton Road, NE
Atlanta, GA 30329
800.ACS.2345
http://www.cancer.org

American Lung Association
1740 Broadway, 14th Floor
New York, NY 10019-4374
212.315.8700
800.LUNG.USA
http://www.lungusa.org

Cancer Care, Inc.
275 Seventh Avenue
New York, NY 10001
212.302.2400
800.813.HOPE
http://www.cancercare.org

National Cancer Institute
Cancer Information Service
800.4.CANCER
http://www.nci.nih.gov

Natural Death Centre
20 Heber Road
London NW2 6AA, UK
0181.208.2853

National Hospice and Palliative Care Organization
1700 Diagonal Road, Suite 300
Arlington, VA 22314
703.837.1500
http://www.nhpco.org

OncoLink
University of Pennsylvania Cancer Center
3400 Spruce Street
2 Donner
Philadelphia, PA 19104
215.349.8895
http://www.oncolink.upenn.edu

Partnership for Caring: America's Voices for the
Dying
1035 30th Street NW
Washington, DC 20007
800.989.WILL
202.338.9790
http://www.partnershipforcaring.org

About the Author

Lois Hjelmstad and her husband, Les, have a daughter, three sons, and twelve grandchildren. She has taught piano, music theory, and composition for forty years.

A year after being diagnosed with chronic fatigue syndrome (CFS), she was diagnosed with breast cancer, followed by a modified radical mastectomy and radiation therapy. The next year, she had a second modified radical mastectomy.

In response to the emotional and physical challenges of those events, she wrote *Fine Black Lines: Reflections on Facing Cancer, Fear and Loneliness.*

Fine Black Lines opened doors for Lois to speak about breast cancer issues. She has given hundreds of presentations throughout the United States, as well as in Canada and England.

Her topics include:

- Breast Cancer and the Issues of Intimacy
- Writing as a Means of Healing
- Cancer as a Catalyst for Change
- Road to Renewal—Reality and Risk
- Mourning My Mother

In addition to teaching, writing, and speaking, Lois loves walking, traveling, entertaining family and friends, being involved with children, and thinking about the larger questions of life.

Her mission is to bring clarity, validation, and solace to others.

About *Fine Black Lines*

In 1990, the night before her first mastectomy, Lois Hjelmstad penned a poem, "Good-bye, Beloved Breast." It was the beginning of the book, *Fine Black Lines: Reflections on Facing Cancer, Fear and Loneliness.*

Lois certainly did not intend to write a book. She was simply searching for courage, comfort, and a sense of certainty about what she had to do. A farewell poem for her radiation therapists followed. She shared the first twenty poems she had written about her cancer experience with her oncologist, who said, "You have to do something with these."

Nine months later, when new symptoms appeared and new decisions were required, a sense of urgency propelled her to resume work on the project. In 1993, she published *Fine Black Lines.* It has been reprinted many times.

Fine Black Lines has brought hope and a new capacity for joy to thousands of women in the United States, Canada, and England.

Index

Titled Prose

Order Information

The Last Violet and *Fine Black Lines* are available through your local bookstore, on amazon.com, or directly from the publisher:

Mulberry Hill Press

2710 S. Washington Street, Suite B

Englewood, CO 80110

800.294.4714

Fine Black Lines	14.95	each book
The Last Violet	14.95	each book
In Colorado, add	.45	each book (sales tax)
Shipping and Handling	5.00	each order

Send name, address, and MC/Visa number with expiration date or check payable to Mulberry Hill Press.

Phone orders: 800.294.4714 or 303.781.8974

Fax orders: 303.806.9313

E-mail orders: hjelmstd@csd.net

Visit website: www.mulberryhillpress.com

If you are interested in having the author read or speak to a group, please contact Mulberry Hill Press at 303.781.8974.